PRIMER OF GREEK LITERATURE

PRIMER OF
GREEK LITERATURE

SIR RICHARD C. JEBB

PREFACE BY
MOHIT K. RAY

ATLANTIC
PUBLISHERS & DISTRIBUTORS

Published by
ATLANTIC PUBLISHERS AND DISTRIBUTORS
B-2, Vishal Enclave, Opp. Rajouri Garden, New Delhi-110027
Phones : 5413460, 5429987, 5466842

Sales Office
4215/1, Ansari Road, Darya Ganj, New Delhi-110002
Phones : 3273880, 3285873, 3280451
Fax : 91-11-3285873
web : www.atlanticbooks.com
e-mail : info@atlanticbooks.com

ISBN 81-269-0190-X

Typeset at
APD Computer Graphics, Delhi
Printed in India at
Nice Printing Press, Delhi

Preface

There is an old saying that art of tragedy died with the Greeks and even Shakespeare could not revive it. The entire European literature owes a grėat deal to the Greeks who were the first in the Western hemisphere to develop the literary forms such as epic, lyric and dramatic poetry, the chief types of prose such as historical, philosophical and oratorial, and we are so much used to these forms that we take them for granted, as something existing in the nature of things. Greek literature, though extremely fascinating in itself, is the ultimate source of all Western literatures. It is a highly rewarding and sustaining experience to enter the world of Greek literature with no less a person than Sir Richard C. Jebb, the profoundest Greek scholar of his time who may be said to hold the Greek literature in the palm of his hand.

The Primer of Greek Literature, originally published in 1877 is divided into three parts. The Part I introduces us to the early literature where Sir Jebb acquaints us in his inimitably lucid style with the rational energy of the Greeks who made reason the guide of their social life, the bearing of Greek thought on modern life, originality of Greek literature, the Greeks' insistence on form, and general course of Greek literature and its natural growth without having any models to follow and an account of the legendary bards like Orpheus. It is interesting to know that the name Orpheus is the Greek name for Indian Ribhu. Then the various kinds of poetry—epic, elegiac, iambic and lyric—are discussed with fine precision. The Part II focuses on the Attic literature where Sir Jebb takes us to the world of Aeschylus, Sophocles and Euripides where the only law worked out both by the gods and the mortals is the law of righteousness. It shows how while Aeschylus is interested in the awful supernatural powers, Sophocles is essentially a dramatist of human character and Euripides brings us to the domestic world of man-woman relationships. In the second chapter of the same part Sir Jebb tells us about the rise of History and we learn a good deal about Herodotus, an intimate friend of Sophocles, Thucydides whom Sir Jebb considers the first philosopher of History, Xenophon and others. Since the development of Attic prose is seen most clearly in the history of Attic oratory, Sir Jebb offers a fine exposition of great orators like Antiphon, Lysias, Isocrates, Idaeus, Demosthenes, Lycurgus and others. In philosophy, we learn a great deal about the basic tenets of Plato, Aristotle, the Epicureans and the Stoics. Part III of the book is concerned mainly with the literature of decadence, of the Alexandrian period and the Graeco-Roman period. Finally, Sir Jebb arrives at the intellectual conviction that from "Rome, along with a noble literature, the modern world derives a continuous tradition of law and government: from Greece it traces the ancient lineage and the still fresh inspirations of an intellectual and spiritual life."

Any student of ancient European classics will find this book, a mine of information and the finest introduction to the world of the Greeks, extremely useful. And since Sir Jebb carries his scholarship lightly and is never pedantic, anybody interested in Greek civilization and culture will also find this book quite interesting.

Dr. K.R. Gupta, Managing Director, Atlantic Publishers and Distributors, New Delhi, deserves our special thanks for making this book available to our students of ancient European classics by bringing out a reprint of the book.

MOHIT K. RAY

CONTENTS

PART I—THE EARLY LITERATURE

1

Introduction

1. A Primer of Greek Literature should aim at being useful, not only to students of Greek, but also to those who do not know Greek, and who will never read a Greek book except in a translation. The civilized world is agreed in holding the great literature of old Greece to be one of the most precious things that have come down from the past, and all educated people, whether they know Greek or not, may naturally wish to know something about the contents of Greek literature. This sketch is intended to serve as a framework into which those who read any of the Greek books, whether in the original or in English, may fit what they read. The unity of Greek Literature is not the unity of a library but the unity of a living body. In this, more perhaps than in any other literature, we shall fail really to understand any one part unless we see clearly what it has to do with the rest. But first—Can we point to any broad characteristics which at once give Greek literature a worth and interest of its own for modern life?

2. **The Rational Energy of the Greeks.** The Greeks were not the first people who found out how to till the earth well, or to fashion metals, or to grow rich by war or commerce, or to build splendid houses and temples. But they were the first people who tried to make reason the guide of their social life. One proof of this is found in the very existence of the Greek cities. While other men were living in tribes or under despotic

kings, the Greeks had already gathered themselves together in cities,—societies ruled, not by force, but by the persuasions of equal law. Another proof of it is found in the Greek books. There we find writers of all sorts, poets and historians and philosophers, habitually striving to get at the reasons of things. On this side, Greek literature has an interest such as belongs to no other literature. It shows us how men first set about systematic thinking. It shows us how some questions which have been solved since, and others which are being discussed still, appeared to the people who first seriously tried to answer them.

3. **The Bearing of Greek Thought on Modern Life.** But the Greek books are not merely interesting as showing the methods and aims of early thinkers. They contain results, too, which have had the deepest and widest influence on the whole of modern life, in religion, in morality, in science, in politics, in literature. The thoughts of the great Greek thinkers have been bearing fruit in the world ever since they were first uttered. In some special sciences, the work done by the Greeks remains a basis of study to this day, as in Ethics and in Logic and in Geometry. It is in Greek historians and Greek orators that we read some of the political lessons most directly useful for our own time. Neither the history of Christian doctrine, nor the outer history of the Christian Church, can be fully understood without reference to the character and work of the Greek mind. Under the influence of Christianity, two principal elements have entered into the spiritual life of the modern world: one of these has been Hebrew; the other has been Greek.

4. **Originality of Greek Literature.** The chief types of poetry, such as the epic, lyric, dramatic,—the chief types of prose, such as the historical, philosophical, oratorical—are so much a matter of course now that we are apt to think of them as existing in the nature of things. But some of them did not exist at all, and others existed only in rude germs, when the Greek genius began its work. One after another, as the need of expression in each kind was felt, each of these types was perfected by the creative

force of that Greek genius. In Greek literature, then, we have not merely a literature very interesting in itself: we have the fountain-head of all Western literature. The influence of Rome on modern literature has in some cases been more direct than that of Greece. But if the influence is tracked to its spring, any broad stream of it will carry us back to a Greek source.

5. **Form.** The Greeks were a physically beautiful race, with great quickness and fineness of perception, which made them feel at once when anything was exaggerated or absurd, or, as we say in bad taste. One of their favourite maxims was, 'Do nothing too much.' They were naturally obedient in all things to a sense of fitness and measure,—what they called *kairos*, a word which means literally 'precision,' the instinct of drawing the line, as it were, at the right place. So when they built a temple, this instinct kept them from making one part of it too large in proportion to another, or from adding ornament in the wrong place: and this is the reason why such a building as the Parthenon at Athens, with its noble simplicity and symmetry, is so perfect of its kind. Or if a Greek made a statue, not only did he make the limbs and features on just the right scale for each other, but he refrained from trying to make the stone express more than it fitly could, or do duty for a picture. In the same way, when they wrote books, the Greeks were guided by their sense of fitness. They felt that it was out of proportion, and therefore ugly, in the words were grander or rarer than the thoughts, and that a style which might be fitting in one kind of composition would be out of place in another. Above all, the Greeks felt that a writer ought to be *clear*, and that any elaborate putting together of words which does not make the thought clear is worse even than misplaced finery. So, in the best work of Greek writers, we generally find these two things. First, the style is of the right kind for the subject; in poetry, for instance, the epic style is kept distinct from the lyric; historical prose is not written like oratory. Secondly, the writer tries to be clear. He chooses the words for the thoughts, he does not enslave the thoughts to the words.

6. **Greek Literature and the Study of Language.** The Greeks excelled, as we have seen, in an instinct for beauty, and in the power of creating beautiful forms: and, of all the beautiful things which they created, their own language was the first and the most wonderful. The Greek mind was very bright and keen, and was accustomed to feeling fine distinctions and light shades of meaning. And so the Greeks gradually moulded their language so that it could express these fine distinctions and light shades by very simple means, and yet with perfect accuracy. By using one turn of phrase instead of another which would have been equally correct, or with the help of those little words called 'particles' which answered to the play of feature or tone of voice in talking, or even by a slight change in the order of the sentence, a Greek could mark with delicate precision the meaning which he meant to convey. This peculiar power which the language acquired of being easily *bent* into the exact shape of the thought entitles Greek to be called the most *flexible* of languages. Grammars give classified examples of this flexibility. But as the fields are better for a botanist than the best collection of dried flowers, so we must go to the Greek books if we would see the language in the fullness of its elastic life. No one who is a stranger to Greek literature has seen how perfect an instrument it is possible for human speech to be.

7. **General Course of Greek Literature.** Greek has lived on from the days before Homer into our own, one and the same language always, in spite of small changes,—still giving new proofs of its flexibility in the ease with which it finds terse expression for modern ideas. And this undying language has never ceased to have a literature; a rude and scanty literature, indeed, it was during one part of its modern course, yet even then lit up now and again by the enthusiasm of Greek scholars for the old Greek genius. This long and still vigorous life has had three great stages: 1. The **Old** Literature, from Homer to 529 A.D., when the Schools of heathen Philosophy were closed by the edict of the Emperor Justinian; 2. The **Middle** or Byzantine

Literature, from 529 A.D. to the capture of Constantinople by the Turks (1453 A.D.); 3. The **Modern** Literature, of which the first beginning may be taken from the satirical poetry, in the popular dialect, of the monk Theodorus Prodromus (1143—1180 A.D.) in the reign of the Emperor Manuel Comnenus. At the end of the last century, the Greek patriot and scholar Koraes helped, by his example, to purify the literary dialect from many corrupt forms and foreign words.

8. **The Old Literature.** We have to do here with the Old Literature only. It may be sub-divided into the Early Literature; the Attic Literature; and the Literature of the Decadence.

I. The **Early Literature** begins with Homer and extends down to about 475 B.C. Epic Poetry flourishes. Elegiac, Iambic and Lyric Poetry arise. Prose writing, though in a rude form, begins among the Ionian Greeks of Asia Minor.

II. The **Attic Literature** flourishes from about 475 to 300 B.C. Dramatic Poetry reaches its perfection at Athens, both in Tragedy and in Comedy: and the Athenians also perfect a Prose Literature in history, oratory, and philosophical dialogue. The Greek genius has now finished its work of creating beautiful forms: and it has now lost the mainspring of its old energy, political freedom. We pass from the age of *creative* art in verse and prose to the age of *learned* work in letters and science.

III. The **Literature of the Decadence** has two chief periods:

(i) The *Alexandrian* period, from 300 B.C. till Greece became subject to Rome in 146 B.C.

(ii) The *Graeco-Roman* period, from 146 B.C. till the Schools of heathen Philosophy were closed in 529 A.D.

9. **Natural Growth of Greek Literature.** The great literature of Greece was not artificial, but grew naturally out of Greek life. As the year brings violets before roses and ripens one fruit earlier than another, so the golden time of the Greek genius has its seasons, in which first one sort of growth, and then another, blossoms, flowers and fades. A literature which copies foreign

models may begin with any kind of verse or prose, and may have several different kinds in vigour at once. But the Greeks had no models. They invented the styles of poetry and prose which they perfected, one after another. The process of invention went step by step with the development of their mental and social life. Each great branch of the Greek race, as its natural turn came, did that special part in the work which it was fittest to do.

10. The three great branches were the **Aeolian**, the **Dorian** and the **Ionian**. At the time when literary history begins, the chief seats of the **Aeolians** were Thessaly, Boeotia, Aetolia, and Acarnania; in the Peloponnesus, Arcadia, Elis and Achaia; the N.W. coasts of Asia Minor, and the island of Lesbos; and great colonies, such as Croton, in Magna Graecia on the S.E. coast of Italy. The **Dorians** held Argolis, Messenia and Laconia in the Peloponnesus; Corinth and Megara; settlements on the S.W. coasts of Asia Minor; the islands of Crete and Rhodes; Syracuse and other colonies on the E. and S. coasts of Sicily; Tarentum and other colonies in Magna Graecia. The Attic part of the **Ionian** stock possessed Attica and Euboea; Ionians were settled on the W. coast of Asia Minor, between the Aeolians on the north and the Dorians on the south; in the islands of Samos and Chios, and in most of the Aegean islets; and in widely spread colonies, including cities in Italy, Sicily, and on the Euxine.

11. Each of these three branches used its own modification of the Greek language, and this modification was called its **dialect**. The **Aeolic dialect**, suited to a quick, tripping utterance, was truer than any other to the oldest *forms* of the language; but it always remained comparatively poor and rude for literary purposes; and even the Aeolic of Lesbos, where the dialect had been cultivated in poetry, could be described by Athenians of Plato's time as 'a barbarian idiom.' Greek is distinguished among Indo-European languages by the completeness and nicety of its *vowel-system*; and one main distinction between the Greek dialects consisted in their treatment of the vowels. In Aeolic, the

o and *u* sounds prevailed. The **Doric dialect** best preserved the oldest *sounds* of the language; it was a highland dialect, the terse and sinewy speech of a steadfast race, whose grave earnestness was joined to a certain dry humour. In Doric, the broad *a* sound prevailed. The **Ionic dialect** was the smooth, harmonious language of an ease-loving people, gifted with bright and versatile intelligence, educated to the contemplative enjoyment of natural beauty by the climate and scenery of the Aegean coasts and islands, and familiarised with elegant luxury by intercourse with Asiatics and Phoenicians. It was characterised by dislike of all rough combinations, by partiality for the liquid meeting of vowels, and especially by love of the soft *e* sound.

12. The **Attic dialect** was a modified form of the Ionic, representing a happy medium between the too enervated Ionic and the somewhat harsh Doric. In its mature phase, it was the artistic creation of Attic Tragedy, influenced both by the epic language of the Homeric poems and by the choral poetry of the Dorians. Between 475 and 300 B.C. Attic became established as the standard dialect of Greek literature. But the separate life of the Greek cities, the physical partition of Greece Proper by mountain-barriers and far-reaching arms of the sea, and the variety of climate both in Greece and in the scattered Greek settlements, favoured the preservation of the dialects down to late times. All the dialects were successively brought into play by the literary development.

13. First, the **Ionians** in the colonies of Asia Minor,—with their keen feeling for grace of form, their genial sympathy with everything bright and joyous in nature, their delight in adventure, and their pliant, musical language, so well fitted for fluent, eager narrative,—wove the warlike stories of heroes and gods into Epic Poetry. Theirs, too, was Elegiac Poetry, the first slight deviation from the Epic. Then the **Aeolians** of Lesbos, proud, chivalrous, imaginative, sensuous, brought forth the Lyric Song of personal passion in war or love, with that union of fiery strength and tenderness which marked the Aeolic speech. The

Dorians of the Peloponnesus and of the colonies in Sicily and Southern Italy created the Choral Lyric Poetry, to be used at the festivals of cities or princes, or in the worship of the gods: poetry in which the simple and earnest religious faith of the Dorians, their intensely conservative pride in the traditions and institutions of the Dorian State, and their love for the usages of Dorian home-life, were uttered in the broad, massive harmonies of the Dorian speech. Lastly, the most gifted branch of the Ionians, the **Attic** people, with their happy balance of qualities, blended together elements of all the earlier kinds in the most complex and artistic form of all, the Drama; and, as the Greek mind and culture reached their full ripeness, raised Greek Prose from its rude beginnings in Ionia to the varied forms of a mature Prose Literature. The Attic work, both in verse and prose, had a universal stamp: it came from the centre of the Greek spirit, and appealed to all the Greeks.

14. In the earlier poetry and prose, **the dialect employed is determined chiefly by the species of the composition**, rather than by the birthplace of the composer. The epic poets of Ionia gradually formed a diction of their own, Ionic in its general character, but not such Ionic as was commonly spoken. This **epic language of Ionia** came to be borrowed more or less by all poets, whether Ionian by birth or not, who put tales about heroes into verse. Thus it is used, though with some alloy from their native dialects, by the Aeolian epic poet Hesiod and by the Dorian elegiac poet Theognis. And, since this Ionian epic dialect had thus established itself as the proper dialect for *story*, it was used by the earliest writers, philosophers or historians, who set forth their thoughts in prose; as by the historian Herodotus, the native of a Dorian city. The **pure Ionic dialect** was that in which Iambic poetry was first composed; and hence we find some pure Ionic forms retained in the iambic verse of Attic Tragedy. **The Doric dialect**, again, belonged especially to Choral Lyric poetry; it is therefore blended with the epic idiom, and with his own Aeolic, by Pindar; and it enters into the choral songs of Attic Tragedy. **Aeolic** was the chosen dialect of love-

songs, and it is used for this strain by the Dorian poet Theocritus. A poet could vary his dialect to suit different kinds of composition. Theocritus wrote his pastoral poems in Doric; the Attic Tyrtaeus used the Ionian epic dialect for his elegies, but wove Doric forms into his marching-songs. Thus, by a division of labour among the dialects, **the literature gradually brought out all the faculties of the language**, giving free play to each in the way that nature seemed to have marked out for it.

15. **The Art of Writing.** There can be no literature, in any proper sense of the word, without writing. For literature implies fixed form: and, though memory may do great feats, a merely oral tradition cannot guarantee fixed form. The Greeks got their alphabet from the Phoenicians, and at first called the letters 'Phoenician signs.' Now the Greeks had dealings with Phoenician merchants while Sidon was still a great commercial and naval power,—at least as early as 1000 B.C., probably earlier. It seems unlikely that the Greeks, with their bright wits, their quickness in taking hints, and their love of story, should have allowed many centuries to go by before they caught up this art of writing from the Phoenicians, whose shrewdness they keenly appreciated, whose fabrics and works in metal they prized so much, and who were their rivals in trade. The historian Herodotus, about 440 B.C., assumes as a matter of course that the art of writing had been perfectly familiar to the Greeks for many centuries before his time. Herodotus was not a critical antiquarian; but he knew Greek life, he had studied its records, he was an accomplished man and a great traveller: and he would scarcely have taken the very old use of writing for granted, as he everywhere does, if this was not, at least, the general belief of well-informed Greeks in his time. Extant evidence makes it probable that the Greeks knew the art of writing before the forms of the language had been fixed as we find them in the oldest literature. We have, however, no definite allusion to, or example of, writing in Greece that can be put earlier than about 700 B.C.

16. It was only very slowly that a reading public came into existence. Priests and poets were the first who made much use of the art of writing. The temple at Delphi was probably one of its earliest centres. At Athens, in the time of the Peloponnesian War (431— 404 B.C.), there were book-shops in the market-place (the quarter was called the 'book-mart'), and there was an export trade in books. As the manuscripts were copied by slaves, whose labour cost little, these written rolls were tolerably cheap. The temples, and a few students or great men, possessed large collections of volumes.[1] But the first public library of Greek books was that founded by Ptolemy I. (306—285 B.C.) at Alexandria.

17. **The Greek Poetry before Homer—at first religious.** Greek literature begins, for us, with the two Homeric poems, the *Iliad* and the *Odyssey*. But these are not at all like the simple ballad-poetry of other countries. They are works of highly finished art, which could not possibly have been produced until the poetical art had been practised for a long time. We have no remains, however, of Greek poetry before Homer. We can only make out some of the general forms that it must have taken. It is as if English literature began suddenly in the fourteenth century with Chaucer, and nothing was known of Beowulf or Caedmon or the old religious poetry except from a few bare names. The most certain fact about the earliest Greek poetry is that it was closely connected with Greek religion.

18. There was a time when our far-off ancestors, the forefathers of Persians and Hindoos, Greeks and Italians, Celts and Teutons and Slavs, lived together in Central Asia, and worshipped the visible agencies or forms of Nature, such as the Sun, the Dawn, the Earth. Then they came to think of these powers as persons, with human bodies and minds. The Sun became a god who drives his fiery chariot through the heavens; the Dawn, a goddess who lays a rosy finger on the gloom; Earth came to be called the Mother of the gods. But this change did not come all at once. There was a time when they had begun to

speak of the natural powers as persons, and yet had not forgotten that they were really natural powers, and that the personal names were merely signs. There are traces of this phase in the Vedas, or sacred Hymns of the Indian Brahmans, which are older than the Homeric poems, and nearer to the spirit of the ancient religion as it existed before Greeks and Indians had parted from the common stock in Central Asia. We have a trace of the same stage, probably, in some old Greek songs, hardly known to us save by name—such as the song of *Linus*, of *Ialemus*, of *Hylas*. Such songs were usually laments for a beautiful youth, who had met with a violent death. **Linus** (the Argives said) was a boy sprung from gods, who grew up among the sheep-folds, and whom dogs tore to pieces. Thus men mourned the young loveliness of spring, slain by the fierce dog-star Sirius.

19. **Hymns to the Gods.** The Greeks were distinguished by their sense of beautiful form, and especially of beauty in the human form. When they had parted from their kinsmen in Asia, they gradually defined their gods in the clear image of beautiful men and women. They could not have rested content with the shadowy or monstrous shapes of the Indian deities. And they said that these gods or goddesses in human form lived on the top of Mount Olympus, a high mountain with snowy peaks in the north of Thessaly. Bards made Hymns in honour of one or another deity, weaving into them, probably, old allegories or mystic lore which the Greeks had brought with them from Asia. One of the deities thus honoured was **Apollo**, the god of brightness and purity, the lord of music, the giver of prophecy, and the healer. To him especially men sang *paeans* or Songs of Health, when they asked him to help them, or praised him for help given. Another was **Demeter**, Earth the Mother, the giver of grain; the hymns to her praised her bounty, or spoke of her sorrow as she sought her daughter Persephone who had been taken to the dark underworld, or her joy when she found her again. Dionysus was the god of wine, of frolic and revelry, and of every physical rapture which lifts up the spirit of man. Both

Dionysus and Demeter were also associated, in the mystic doctrine, with the idea of a life after death. **Cybele** was the name given by the Phrygians of Asia Minor to the 'Mother of the gods'; she was worshipped, with clashing of cymbals and the music of the flute, and wild dances, by priests called Corybantes.

20. **Legendary Bards.** The earliest poet, in Greek legend, is **Orpheus**. The name of this mythical person is the Greek form of the Indian *Ribhu.* The Ribhus figure in the Indian hymns as great artificers, the first mortals who were raised to the gods. Orpheus, like other early bards, is called *Thracian.* This means that he was connected with the worship of the **Muses**, goddesses who preside over poetry. Their worship was imparted by a people called Thracians to the Greeks in Pieria, a district on the N.E. border of Thessaly, whence it spread southward to Parnassus in Phocis and Helicon in Boeotia. From early times the Greeks connected Orpheus with mystic teaching about the origin of the world and the immortality of the soul, and associated him with the worship of the god Dionysus in the underworld. **Musaeus** ('servant of the Muses'), also 'Thracian,' and sometimes called a disciple of Orpheus, is especially connected with the mystic worship of Demeter at Eleusis in Attica. This worship was said to have been founded by the 'Thracian' **Eumolpus** ('the good chanter), whom the priestly family of the Eumolpidae claimed as their ancestor. The bard **Thamyras** is another of the Thracian group.

21. The first hymns to Apollo were said to have been made by **Olen**, a Lycian, **Chrysothemis,** a Cretan, and **Philammon**, of Delphi. Then we hear also of Phrygian or Cretan bards who made hymns to Cybele, such as **Olympus** the pupil of Marsyas (a demi-god, said to have been vanquished by Apollo in a musical contest), and **Hyagnis.** The age of this earliest sacred poetry must have followed close on the migration of the Greeks from the old common home in Asia. When these early hymns were made, some of the Greeks were still on their way through Thrace and Macedonia, others were settling in the Aegean

islands, others were still in Asia. And so we have three main streams of this early poetry, the '**Thracian**' or Northern, the **Phrygian**, and the **Cretan**.

22. **The Marriage-Hymn.** *The dirge*—The Homeric *Iliad* mentions the joyous marriage-hymn, sung as the bridegroom brings the bride home; and the dirge or *thrēnus* for the dead. Now in ancient India both of these were chanted by the priest as part of a solemn ritual. And so it must once have been with the Greeks. But, when the *Iliad* was composed, both marriage-song and dirge had acquired a free, popular form. Here we see the early tendency of the Greeks to **divest song of its character as part of a liturgy, and to make it secular**, the work of the lay artist, for all the people.

Note

1. Among the oldest Greek manuscripts now extant are some Egyptian papyri, part of them as old perhaps as 160 B.C., including fragments of Homer's Iliad and of the orator Hypereides, and some rolls from Herculaneum (a town which was destroyed in 79 A.D.), containing writings of the Epicurean philosopher Philodêmus, a contemporary of Cicero. A parchment at Milan, with fragments of the Iliad, is of the 4th or 5th century A.D. The 'Sinaitic' ms. of the New Testament is of the 5th century or earlier: the Vatican ms. is of the 4th. With these and one or two more exceptions, we have no Greek manuscript older than the 9th century A.D. A few of the best, such as the Venice ms. of the Iliad and the Paris ms. of Demosthenes, belong to the 10th century; or, as the Florentine ms. of Aeschylus and Sophocles, and the Ravenna ms. of Aristophanes, to the 11th century. From the 12th century onwards the mss. are more abundant. The first book printed in Greek type was the Greek grammar of Constantine Lascaris (Milan, 1476): the first Greek author, Aesop's Fables (Milan, 1479). Homer's Iliad and Odyssey were first printed at Florence in 1488. By 1550 most of the Greek classics had been printed, chiefly by the Aldi at Venice, Junta at Florence, and Stephanus at Paris.

2

Epic Poetry

The Homeric *Iliad* and *Odyssey*, 940—850 B.C. The Cyclic Poets, 776—550 B.C. Hesiod, 850—800 B.C. The Homeric *Hymns*, 776—500 B.C.

1. **Songs of Warriors.** *The minstrel*—By the side of the sacred hymns, there must very early have sprung up songs of warriors and brave deeds in war. The *Iliad* makes the heroes at Troy sing such songs, and the *Iliad* and *Odyssey* themselves are built up from very old songs of this kind. The *Odyssey* gives us a lively picture of the *minstrel* (*aoidos*) by whom such songs were sung in the halls of princes. A king is going to make a great feast, and bids his herald, the chamberlain of his court, to invite 'the god-like singer; for to him the god has given song abundantly, to gladden us.' So the chamberlain brings 'the welcome minstrel, whom the Muse loved exceedingly, and to whom she gave both evil and good; she took away his eyesight, but she gave him sweet song'; he sets a chair for the minstrel, studded with silver nails, in the midst of the feasters, firm against a tall pillar, and hangs a clear-toned harp on a peg just above his head, and guides the blind man's hands to touch it: then he puts a table beside him, with food and wine. When the banquet is over, the minstrel sings to his harp 'the glories of men.' Such a minstrel was not looked upon simply as an artist; he was thought to be inspired by the gods. And so, naturally, he had a sacred character. When King Agamemnon was going away to the war at Troy (the story said) he charged the minstrel of his house to watch over the honour of the queen

Clytaemnestra: and at first the wicked Aegisthus was baffled, 'for the lady was discreet; and, besides, the minstrel was present.'

2. **Epic Poetry.** These songs, sung to the harp by minstrels, were the beginnings out of which *Epic Poetry* was slowly shaped by a long series of poets. '*Epic*' is from the Greek *epos*, ' a saying' or 'word,'—connected, through its root *vep*, with the Latin *vox*, 'voice,' and with the *vi* of 'invite.' *Epos* came to be used especially of an oracle, since a god's answer was the most important sort of 'saying.' Then, as oracles came to be given in verse, *epos* came to mean 'a verse': and the plural, *epê*, 'verses,' could be used either of poetry generally or of a single poem. Later, when lyric songs set to music were called *melê*, 'things sung,' all poems which were not accompanied by music, but merely recited, were distinguished as *epê*, '*spoken* verses.' Now the chief kind of poetry which was thus merely recited was, like the Homeric, *narrative poetry in hexameter verse*. To this kind, therefore, the name *epê* was especially given, and it came to be called *Epic Poetry*. Hexameter verse—called 'heroic' verse by the Greeks, because it was used in epic poetry which tells of heroes—is known to English readers from such poems as Longfellow's *Evangeline*, Kingsley's *Andromeda*, Clough's *Bothie*.

According to Aristotle, the story of an epic poem must be on a *great* and noble theme: it must be *one* in itself; and it must be *complete*, that is, it must have a regular development from the beginning to the end. Epic poetry is the only extant Greek poetry older than about 700 B.C. In the later days of the literature we meet with artificial or learned epics. But at present we have to do with the early or original epic poetry. This is represented by the Homeric *Iliad* and *Odyssey*; the fragments of the Cyclic Poets; the Poems of Hesiod; and the Homeric Hymns.

3. **The Story of the *Iliad*.** The *Iliad* means the *Poem of Ilion* or *Troy*, a city of Mysia in the north-west of Asia Minor. The subject of the poem is one chapter of events in the ten years' siege of Troy by the Greeks. Paris (also called Alexander), son of Priam king of Troy, had carried off Helen, the fairest of women,

wife of Menelaus, king of Sparta. Helen had been wooed by many suitors, and her father Tyndareus had bound them all by an oath to join in avenging that man whom she should marry, if she were taken from him by force. So Agamemnon, king of Mycenae, called together these suitors and other chieftains from all parts of Greece, and they sailed with many ships to besiege Troy. For ten years they besieged it in vain, though the Trojans dared not come out and fight pitched battles; for there was a hero in the Greek army so terrible that not even Hector, the greatest of the Trojan warriors, could stand before him. This hero was Achilles, whom the sea-goddess Thetis had borne to Peleus, king of Phthiôtis, in Thessaly. But at last, in the tenth year of the siege, Achilles suffered a grievous affront from the king Agamemnon, who took away from him his prize, the captive damsel Brisêis. Then Achilles was angry and said that he would fight for the Greeks no more, and withdrew from the army to his tent by the sea-shore.

4. This is the moment at which the *Iliad* begins. 'Sing, goddess, the wrath of Achilles.' The Wrath of Achilles—what it did, and how at last it was turned away—is the central subject of the *Iliad*. But this subject is so treated as to make a general picture of the whole siege during a few days of its tenth and last year, when Troy was about to fall. The first result of Achilles refusing to fight was that the Trojans now dared to come forth and give battle to the Greeks. The *Iliad* is in 24 books. The first 15 of these are taken up with the story of the wavering strife; how victory leaned now this way, now that; how some Greek hero slew a Trojan hero hand to hand, or a Trojan slew a Greek; how the gods and goddesses themselves took this or that side in the fray. But at last the Greeks are hard pressed. Then Patroclus, the friend of Achilles, pleads with him: 'O dreadful in thy prowess! What good will any one have of thee in days to come, unless thou turn away foul ruin from the Greeks ?' Still Achilles will not fight. But he lends his armour to Patroclus, so that his friend may be taken for him, and allows him to lead forth his followers, the Myrmidons. Patroclus is slain by Hector. Then, at last,

Achille is roused. He rushes to the field, drives the Trojans within their walls, and slays Hector, the last hope of Troy, and drags his body, tied to his chariot, back to the ships. The *Iliad* ends with king Priam coming to ask the body of his slain son from Achilles. 'I have borne,' the old man says, 'what no one on the earth has ever borne—to lift to my lips the hands of the man who has slain my son.' Achilles grants his prayer, and there is a truce while the people of Troy pay the last rites to Hector.

5. The Story of the *Odyssey*. The *Odyssey* means the *Poem of Odysseus* (or, as the Romans called him, Ulysses), who was the king of the island of Ithaca, and the cleverest of all the Greek princes who fought against Troy. When Troy was taken, Odysseus and his followers sailed for Ithaca. But on their way they were driven to the land of the *Cyclôpes,* a savage race of one-eyed giants; and here Odysseus put out the eye of the Cyclops Polyphêmus, after that monster had eaten six of the hero's comrades. Now Poseidon, the god of the sea, was the father of Polyphêmus; and Poseidon, in revenge, doomed Odysseus to wander far and wide over the sea to strange lands. When the *Odyssey* begins, it is ten years since the fall of Troy, and Odysseus is still far away from home in the island of *Ogygia,* at the centre of the sea. For seven years the nymph Calypso ('Concealment'), who loves him, has detained him there against his will. Meanwhile his wife Penelope, in Ithaca, has been courted by more than a hundred suitors, lawless, violent men, who feast riotously in the house of Odysseus, as if it were their own. She tried to gain time by pretending that she wished to finish a fine winding-sheet, which she was weaving, before she made her choice; and every night she took down what she had woven by day. But when she had done thus for three years, the suitors found out the trick, and became more urgent thán, ever. And now Telemachus, the son of Odysseus, is urged by the friendly goddess Athene to go in search of his father to Pylus, in the Peloponnesus, where he is entertained by king Nestor, and then to Sparta, where he is the guest of king Menelaus.

6. Here our story goes back to Odysseus. The god Hermes tells Calypso from Zeus that she must let him go, and she obeys. Odysseus sails from her island on a sort of raft which he has made for himself. His old enemy, the sea-god Poseidon, presently espies him, and wrecks his raft: but a sea-goddess, Ino, gives him a magic scarf which buoys him up, and he comes safe to the island of the Phaeacians, a rich and happy people near to the gods and famous as seamen whose orchards bear fruit all the year round. The king Alcinous entertains Odysseus, who relates all his strange adventures; how (before he came to Calypso's isle) he and his companions visited the isle of the enchantress Circê, who changed the others into swine, while he himself was saved by a charmed herb called *moly*, and persuaded her to restore his friends to the human form; how they passed by the shore of the sweet-singing Sirens, and between Scylla and Charybdis; and how at last all his comrades perished because they had slain the sacred oxen of the Sun-god.

7. Then a Phaeacian crew take Odysseus back to Ithaca in a ship. His faithful swineherd Eumaeus does not know him, for Athene has disguised him as an old beggar-man; but his old dog Argus knows his master, who has been twenty years away; he wags his tail and drops his ears as the beggar-man comes near, and dies. Meanwhile Telemachus comes back from his search. Athene reveals his father to him, and father and son arrange a plan of vengeance on the suitors. Odysseus, still disguised, has an audience of Penelope, pretending to bring news of her husband, but narrowly escapes being discovered through his old nurse Eurycleia recognising a scar as she is washing his feet. Penelope, inspired by Athene, now says that she will wed that suitor who can send an arrow from the bow of the hero Eurytus—an heirloom in the house—through the helve-holes of twelve pole-axes put one behind another in the hall. Not one of the suitors can even string the bow. But the disguised Odysseus bends it easily, and sends an arrow clean through the holes. This is the signal for the slaughter of the suitors. Odysseus showers his arrows on them, and finally, helped by Telemachus

and two trusty servants, slays them all. Now at last he reveals himself to his wife, and tells her the story of his journeys. The 24th book tells how the god Hermes led the shades of the suitors beneath the earth; how Odysseus in Ithaca was made known to his father Laertes; how he overcame the kinsfolk of the suitors who sought to avenge them; and how he was reconciled to his people.

8. **The Two Heroes.** Achilles and Odysseus are two characters which always had a strong hold upon the Greek imagination. The Greek idea of human perfection was a wise mind in a beautiful body, good counsel joined to noble action. Noble action is preeminently represented by Achilles, good counsel by Odysseus. Odysseus is brave, but he is especially the man of subtle intellect and ready resource. It was a grave fault of the Greeks that they cared too little whether that quickness of wit which they so much admired was or was not honest. It is not strange that the noble Homeric conception of Odysseus should have been lowered by later Greek poets, who, dwelling chiefly on his subtlety, sometimes made him an unscrupulous knave, reckless of everything except personal gain.

No such shadow ever fell on the Homeric Achilles. His irresistible might and splendour in war, his stormy human passions, his fine sense, fitting in the son of a goddess, for what is soothing or strengthening in the messages of the gods, his love passing the love of women, his foresight of an early death, even when life was most dazzling, made him glow before the Greek imagination with an immortal youth, as the very type of chivalry in their race. The early ambitions of Alexander the Great were fired by this Homeric vision of Achilles. Nothing can show better how vividly the Homeric Poems wrought in Greek life and history than to see how real the young Greek hero at Troy was to the young Greek conqueror of the East.

9. **Homeric Theology.** The *Odyssey* bears the marks of a later time than the *Iliad.* Still, there is a general agreement between the two poems in the broad features of the age which

they describe. Each poem is a picture of an heroic age on which the poet looks back as far-off in the past, but for his idea of which he draws in some measure on his own days. The deities of the *Iliad* are colossal men and women, stronger and fairer than mortals, able to work wonders and to take any form they please, but not all-powerful or all-wise, and often immoral. They dwell on the snow-crowned mountain Olympus, and are called the Olympian gods. Zeus, a sensual, passionate, but genial person (Jupiter the sky), is their chief, having overthrown the dynasty of his father Cronus (Saturn), which preceded the Olympian dynasty. Next to Zeus are four great deities,—Herê, his queen, with whom he quarrels much; Apollo; Athene (who represents especially intelligence); and Poseidon, god of the sea. Other gods sometimes dispute the supremacy of Zeus, and he quells them by threats or by force. The gods act on man chiefly by hurting or comforting his body in some way, and expect from him offerings of savoury food and wine. In the *Odyssey* we find a more spiritual conception. Olympus has become a shadowy far-off place, where the gods dwell apart. Zeus is now indisputably supreme. The gods now act not only on man's body, but also, and chiefly, on his mind and heart. They also wander over the earth in disguise, spying out who are just among men. The Homeric poems did much towards establishing a fixed standard type for each deity, and reconciling the inconsistencies of different local worships. But they did not *create* this theology, which was far older.

10. **Homeric Morality.** The Homeric gods punish a man for disobeying or affronting them in any way; but they do not always punish him for immoral actions. Fear of the gods, then, though powerful as far as it goes, would not go very far towards making the Homeric man moral. For that he needs a moral law, independent of his religion. Among the warriors of the *Iliad*, such a law is represented chiefly by what the Greeks call *aidôs*, and which is often nearly what we call the sense of honour. Along with this, there is another principle which comes out more clearly in the *Odyssey* than in the *Iliad*. This is *nemesis*,

literally 'distribution,' then, that feeling which is roused in the mind by an unjust distribution,—moral indignation. A man feels *aidôs* for the opinion of his neighbours. He feels *nemesis* when his own sense of right is shocked. In the *Odyssey* we find a riper moral sense than in the *Iliad*, and a much larger number of words to express moral distinctions. The age of reflection has begun, as the bits of proverbial philosophy in the *Odyssey* show. Homeric morality is high relatively to Homeric religion: but, as a rule, the Homeric man recognises duties, not towards his fellow-creatures as such, but only towards certain classes of them, who stand in a special relation to himself, as masters, or dependents, or guests, or suppliants.

11. **Homeric Politics.** The Homeric Poems give us the earliest sketch of certain political principles which may be traced through every branch of the Indo-European family of nations. Homeric political life has three great elements—King, Council and Assembly,—the germs of Monarchy, Aristocracy, Democracy. The Homeric King (*Basileus*) leads his people in war, he is supreme judge, and he takes the chief part in public sacrifices to the gods,—but only as the head of the family does in a private sacrifice: the king is not a priest. He rules by divine right. The gods have given to his house that sceptre which he received from his father, and which he will hand on to his son. But his power is limited in three ways. First, he must obey certain customs and traditions of his people, which form a body of unwritten yet positive law (*themistes*), and are the basis on which public justice is administered. Secondly, he must consult his Council (*Boulê*) of nobles and elders. Thirdly, his proposed measures must have the sanction of his whole people in their Assembly (*Agora*). The commoners who make up this Assembly cannot originate or discuss measures, they can only vote Aye or No. The saucy Thersîtes in the *Iliad* attempts to make a blustering speech, but sits down whimpering with a red weal on his back from the staff of Odysseus. In the *Odyssey* some critics have seen a time when the Assembly was beginning to play more than this passive part, and when, on the other hand, the king's

successor was not necessarily his son or heir, but might be one of the nobles who were now more nearly on a level with him.

12. **Homeric Manners** are the social side of Homeric politics. The public life is monarchical. The social life is patriarchal. As the king cares for his subjects, so the patriarch cares for his dependents. The intercourse of the chiefs is marked by the courtesy of a noble warrior caste, strangely mingled with brutal ferocity. Achilles is the model of Greek knighthood. His reception of the king Priam is worthy of a knight. Yet even then Achilles feels the wild beast within him: he dreads lest, at some rash word, his fury should leap out, and he should slay his helpless old guest. A tie of hospitality (*xenia*) or hereditary friendship is held to exist between men whose fathers have entertained each other, and this claim ensures a welcome. Hospitality to all wayfarers is recognised as a duty, since 'strangers and beggars are sent by Zeus'; but a man who really 'welcomed all comers' is named in the *Iliad* as if his virtue was memorable. Women have a higher position and more freedom than in the later historical age of Greece. Polygamy is unknown among Greeks, and there are few exceptions to the sanctity of marriage. The home-life of King Alcinous and Queen Arêtê in the *Odyssey* is like a modern picture of fireside happiness, and no image of girlhood more noble or charming than Nausicaa can be found in poetry. A touch in the *Iliad* shows real feeling for the pathos of a lonely woman's life—the mention of the 'true-hearted toiler,' working all day long 'to win a scanty wage for her children.'

13. The amusements of a chief's country life are hunting, farming or gardening, playing at games such as throwing the javelin or quoit, or, after a solid but temperate dinner, listening to the minstrel's song. The mistress of the house weaves or embroiders among her handmaids. Queen Arêtê had made the robe which Nausicaa gave to Odysseus: and the princess helped her mother in household matters, being in sole charge of the washing. Slaves were often of gentle birth and nurture, having

been taken in war or kidnapped in childhood; the latter was the case with Eumaeus, the trusty swineherd of Odysseus; and we see here how intimate might be the confidence between master and old retainer. The *Iliad* gives us some bright glimpses of simple, joyous life: the patriarchal chief standing silent, glad at heart, among his reapers, while food is being made ready under the trees; the troop of vintagers bearing the baskets of grapes with dance and song from the vineyard; the bridal procession, with the marriage-hymn sounding and the bridegroom's friends dancing to flute and harp while the women stand at their doors to see it pass; the maidens, with their fine linen robes and fair diadems, the youths with glossy tunics and golden swords slung by silver belts, dancing to the minstrel's music, while a delighted crowd looks on.

14. **Homeric Arts and Knowledge.** One test of civilisation is the material of which men make their implements. Stone comes before metal. But the metal age itself has periods. In the first period, men use the metals separately, or hammer them together, but do not know how to smelt or fuse or solder them. The Homeric poems belong to the end of this first period. The next step is usually the smelting of copper with tin, so as to make bronze. The metals named come thus in Homeric order of value:— (1) gold; (2) silver; (3) tin; (4) iron; (5) copper (*chalcus* certainly not 'brass,' *i.e.* copper + zinc), (6) lead. 'Cyanus' was probably a blue glass paste (artificial lapis lazuli). Fine works in metal are usually of Phoenician workmanship,—as armour (cuirass, shield, helmet),—bowls and vases,—ornamental baskets,—clasps, brooches, necklaces, & c. There is no money. A fine can be paid in gold and copper; 'two talents' weight of gold' are once mentioned as a gift of honour; but oxen are the only regular measure of value. A mad bargain is to exchange armour worth 100 oxen for armour worth 9: a precious daughter is one 'who brings oxen' (to her parents, in dower from her suitor). There is no certain allusion to writing; in *Iliad* VII. 172 the heroes scratch their marks on their lots; but in VI. 172 the

'signs' on the 'folded tablet' are perhaps alphabetical. In any case, we need not assume that the poet could not write himself. In the *Odyssey* we hear of 'professional men'—physicians, soothsayers, minstrels, heralds, artificers in wood and metal.

15. The earth is imagined as a sort of flat oval, with the river Oceanus flowing round it. The poet of the *Iliad* knows the coasts of Asia Minor and their islands, but describes no scenery in Greece Proper, and knows the lands to east and south only from hearsay. The poet of the *Odyssey* had probably never seen Ithaca or its neighbouring islands, but knew the Peloponnesus and the eastern parts of Greece Proper. Cyprus (whence 'copper') is mentioned in both poems. The Nile is 'the river Egypt.' Egyptian Thebes is the type of a rich and glorious place—ranking with Orchomenus in Boeotia and (for wealth) with Delphi. Its old greatness under Ramses was long past: Memphis was the capital when these poets sang: but Thebes had been embelished by Sesonchis, founder of the 22nd Egyptian dynasty, and the fame of his march into Syria may have reached Ionian poets of 930—900 B.C. Sidon, capital and seaport of Phoenicia, is famous for embroidery and metal work. Tyre is never named.

16. **Homer.** The Greeks themselves, and all men till the end of the last century, were nearly unanimous in believing the *Iliad* and the *Odyssey* to be the work of one poet, Homer. Homer is named in a spurious fragment of Hesiod, but the earliest authentic mention is in the philosopher and poet Xenophanes, who flourished about 510 B.C. The name Homêrus means 'fitted together,' and was the ordinary word for a *hostage,* i.e. a pledge *agreed upon* between two parties. But nothing was accurately known about his life or date. Most opinions placed Homer either in the time when the Ionian colonies in Asia Minor were founded (about 1044 B.C.), or within a century later. The philosopher Aristotle, who wrote on Homer, and the Homeric critic Aristarchus, seem to have put him about 1044 B.C. The historian Herodotus (440 B.C.) differing, probably, from most of his own contemporaries, made Homer, along with Hesiod, live

as late as 850 B.C. According to a Greek epigram, Homer was claimed as son by Smyrna, Chios, Colophon, Ithaca, Pylus, Argos, Athens. But all the best evidence connects Homer with **Smyrna,** an originally Aeolian city which afterwards became Ionian. An ancient epithet for him is *Melesigenes,* 'son of Meles,' the name of a stream which flowed through old Smyrna, on the border between Aeolis and Ionia. This is significant when we remember that the *Iliad* is an Ionian poem on Aeolian themes. The unknown author of the 'Homeric' Hymn to Apollo of Delos speaks of himself as a blind old man living in Chios: the ancients thought that this Hymn was by Homer, and thus the tradition of Homer's blindness was perpetuated. The little island Ios, one of the Cyclades, claimed to have Homer's grave. **Homeridae,** 'Sons of Homer,' who claimed to be descendants of the poet, lived in the Ionian island of **Chios.** It has been thought that the epic art was hereditary in their house; but this is doubtful. In Plato, 'Homeridae' seem to be merely 'students of Homer.'

17. **Early History of the Homeric Poems.** Both *Iliad* and *Odyssey* had their first origin on the Ionian coast of Asia Minor, and came thence to Greece Proper. The Spartans said that their lawgiver Lycurgus first brought to Greece a complete copy of the Poems, which he had got from the *Creophylidae,* a family of poets in Samos. Athens was of small account when the *Iliad* was first sung: the poem mentions it only once, as 'a well-built town,' and the only one of Athenian warriors who is mentioned by name is quite obscure. But it was at Athens, not at Sparta, that loving care for the poems was first shown in Greece Proper. The traditions of this care refer to the 6th century B.C., and, connect themselves with three names, the law-giver Solon, the tyrant Peisistratus, and his son Hipparchus.[1] **Peisistratus,** in the last period of his rule (537—527 B.C.), is said to have commissioned some learned men, of whom the poet Onomacritus was the chief, to collect the poems of Homer. It is now generally believed that an *Iliad* and an *Odyssey* already existed in writing at that time, but that the text had become much deranged, especially through the practice of reciting short

passages without regard to their context. Besides these two poems, many other epic poems or fragments of the Ionian school went under Homer's name. The supposed task of the commission was to collect *all* these, 'poems of Homer' into one body. The whole story about this commission rests, however, on very dubious authority. Their work cannot, in any case, have been critical in a modern sense. But it is quite possible that some systematic attempt to preserve 'the poems of Homer' was made in the reign of Peisistratus. And one fact is certain. In the 6th century B.C. reciters of 'Homeric poems' regularly competed for a prize at the greatest of Athenian festivals, the Panathenaea. held in every fourth year.

18. **Rhapsodists.** These reciters were called *rhapsodists.* 'Rhapsodist' means literally 'a stitcher of songs'; hence one who weaves a long, smoothly-flowing chant, *i.e. an epic poet,* as *chanting* his poem in a flowing recitative. The characters of poet and reciter were always united,—first in the early minstrel; then in the hereditary poets, such as the Homeridae; and then in the free guild of poets, the rhapsodists, to whom the name of Homeridae was extended. But the early minstrel sang to the harp: the later 'rhapsodist' merely chanted, with a branch of laurel, the symbol of poetry, in his hand. Those who tell how the people in an Indian village still hang on the lips of him who recites one of the great Indian epics help us to imagine the passionate sympathy, the tears, the rapture, with which a Greek crowd heard it told how the King of Troy knelt to Achilles in his tent by night, or how the dying hound in the court-yard of Odysseus just lived to give a feeble welcome to the wanderer whom no one else knew.

19. **Study of Homer in Greece.** The Homeric poems were to the Greeks more than national poems have ever been to any people. Every other people, as it has grown older, has turned away from the poetry of its youth, or has even allowed it to perish. Cicero mourns the loss of the early Roman lays; the English ballads in Percy's collection are mere gleanings of a

once great harvest; Walter Scott was only in time to save relics from the minstrelsy of the Border. But the Homeric poems were simple and strong enough to be popular early, and mature enough in art to please an age of ripe culture. Boys learned Homer by heart at school, priests quoted him touching the gods, moralists went to him for maxims, statesmen for arguments, cities for claims to territory or alliance, noble houses for the title-deeds of their fame. From about 450 B.C. **'civic' or 'public' editions** were prepared by various cities for their own use at public festivals. There was 'the edition of Massilia,' of Chios, 'of Sinôpê,' 'of Argos,' 'of Cyprus,' 'of Crete.' 'Private editions,' the work of individual revisers, were also numerous. The most famous of these was that prepared by Aristotle for his pupil Alexander,—known as 'the Edition of the Casket' from the jewelled case in which Alexander is said to have carried it about with him in the East.

The learned study of Homer at Alexandria reached its highest point in **Aristarchus** (156 B.C.), whose revision of the text became the standard one, and is mainly the basis of our own. The Alexandrian scholars had no text as old as Peisistratus, and knew little of what his Commission had done; they used mainly the editions of the cities, especially Massilia, Chios, and Argos. The division of *Iliad* and *Odyssey* into 24 books each is older than Aristarchus, but not demonstrably older than Zenodotus (280 B.C.): before, the poems had been divided by 'rhapsodies' or short cantos: thus our Book I of the *Iliad* contained two cantos, 'The Anger' and 'The Plague.' Aristarchus founded a school of Homeric criticism which continued productive till about 200 A.D. All this work is now known only from scanty notices.

20. Our oldest and best manuscript of either poem, the *Venetus* A of the *Iliad,* is of the 10th century, and was found at Venice late in the last century, along with some scholia or commentaries which are of value as preserving remarks of Aristarchus and other Alexandrian scholars. Hitherto it had

been thought that the text of Homer had come down to us from about 1000 B.C. The discrepancies in the Alexandrian copies now became better known. The first printed edition of Homer, revised by the Byzantine Demetrius Chalkondyles (b. 1430, d. 1510), was published at Florence in 1488: the first Aldine Edition at Venice in 1504.

21. **The Homeric Question.** The belief that Homer composed both *Iliad* and *Odyssey* was unquestioned, until, about 170 B.C., a grammarian Hellanicus, and one Xenon, asserted that Homer was the author of the *Iliad* but not of the *Odyssey.* They and their followers were called the **Separaters** (*chôrizontes*), because they separated the *Iliad,* in its origin, from the *Odyssey.* As to their grounds, we only know that one of these was the *style,* and this implies literary study. Old Greece was uncritical, and believed strongly in one author for both poems. The mere fact that a double authorship should have been mooted shows that there were good grounds for a natural doubt. But the doubt found little acceptance. Aristarchus wrote against 'the paradox of Xenon,' and the Roman Seneca, writing 'on the shortness of life,' regards this as a question for which life is *too* short.

Early in the last century Vico, a Neapolitan (b. 1668, d. 1744), in his 'Principles of New Knowledge,' maintained that the names of great lawgivers and poets of the old world are symbols; thus 'Homer' is Greek Epic Poetry; 'Homer's poems' were made by a series of poets, and not written down at first; and the Odyssey is at least a century younger than the Iliad. But Vico had no proofs. These were first offered by **F.A. Wolf** in his *Prolegomena* (1795) or Introduction to his edition of Homer. Neither the *Iliad* nor the *Odyssey,* he says, was originally made as one poem. Each has been put together from many small unwritten poems. These, by different authors, had no common plan. The *Iliad* and *Odyssey* were first framed from these, and first written down, by the Commission of Peisistratus. Wolf's theory—as throwing light on the origin of popular poetry generally—roused enthusiasm in Germany, which was then in literary revolt from art to nature.

22. The result of Homeric study since Wolf has been, not to prove any precise theory, but to gain wider assent for certain propositions which narrow the scope of the question.

The *Iliad* and the *Odyssey* belong to the end, not to the beginning, of a poetical epoch. They mark the highest point reached by a school of poetry in Ionia, which took its first models from the Greece Proper of Achaean days, and gradually perfected a style suited to heroic narrative.

23. The *Iliad* has been enlarged and remodelled, by several hands, from a shorter poem, by one poet, on the Wrath of Achilles. This original ' Wrath of Achilles,' probably composed before 950 B.C., was not merely a short lay, but a poem on a larger plan, in which the central motive gave unity to a varied action, and which might properly be called *epic.* It may have been only the last and best of a lost series of similar poems. But if it was the first of its kind, then its author was the founder of the epic art, who made the advance, not from the primitive war-song to an epic on a grand scale, but from the lay to the short epic. This supposition—that in the series of Ionian poets there came one poet of marked original genius—is favoured by the fixed belief of old Greece in a personal Homer, especially if 'Homer' cannot be explained as a symbolical name.[2]

The *Odyssey* has been put together by one poet, who was of later date than the author of the 'Wrath,' and who used earlier lays about the return of the heroes from Troy. It had taken nearly its present form before 660 B.C.: it has been interpolated, but not so much as the *Iliad,* and its original *plan* has been little altered. Both *Iliad* and *Odyssey* arose on the Ionian coast or its islands, and came thence to Greece Proper: though some later additions to the *Odyssey* may be native to the Peloponnesus.

24. A family, such as the Homeridae, handing down the poetical art from father to son, may have preserved the poems, as precious heirlooms, by memory alone, and tided them over an age in which writing was not yet generally used for literary purposes. If, however, the art of writing was known in Ionia

when the 'Wrath of Achilles' was composed, then it is conceivable that the earliest epic poet should have used it, even though a *popular* literary use of writing may not have come in till much later.

25. **The 'Cyclic' Poets**. There was a mass of songs and legends about Troy which the two great epics left untouched. This material was worked up, between 776 B.C. and 550 B.C., by a number of epic poets of the Ionian school, who aimed at linking their poems with the *Iliad* and *Odyssey* as introductions or continuations. In later times, compilers of mythology used to make abstracts in prose from these epics, taking them in the chronological order of the events, so as to make one connected story. A body of epics, arranged in the chronological order of the subjects, was called an **Epic Cycle** (or circle). There was an 'Epic Cycle,'—when put together, we do not know—of which the ' Trojan Cycle,' or epics concerning Troy, formed one part.

26. The Greek grammarian Proclus (140 A.D.), in his 'Literary Treasury,' tells us the names and subjects of some epics belonging to the **Trojan cycle** of myths. (1) *The Cyprian Lays,* so called from the home of their author, Stasînus, related the preparations for the expedition to Troy, and the first nine years of the siege, thus leading up to the *Iliad.* (2) The *Lay of Aethiopia,* by Arctînus of Miletus, was so called because the Aethiopian prince Memnon was its hero, and continued the *Iliad,* telling how the Amazons came to Troy, how Achilles slew their queen and was himself slain by Paris. (3) The *Sack of Troy,* by the same Arctînus, is a supplement to the last. (4) The *Little Iliad,* by Lesches of Mitylene, continued Homer's *Iliad* down to the fall of Troy, giving especial prominence to Ajax and Philoctetes. (5) The *Homeward Voyages,* by Agias of Troezên, filled up the interval of 10 years between the Homeric *Iliad* and *Odyssey* with the adventures of various heroes immediately after the end of the war. (6) The *Lay of Telegonus* (*Telegonia*), by Eugammon of Cyrene, one of the latest of these epic poets (about 566 B.C.),

told how Telegonus, son of the enchantress Circe by Odysseus, was sent by her to seek his father, and slew him in Ithaca.

There was also a **Theban cycle** of myths, to which belonged the *Thebais* (author unknown), relating a war, earlier than the Trojan, between Argos and Thebes, and the *Epigoni* or 'Descendants,' telling of its renewal by the sons of the former warriors. The latter, like the *Cyprian Lays* and other epics, was ascribed to Homer in the time of Herodotus. The *Taking of Oechalia* belonged to a circle of myths about Heracles. These so-called Cyclic poems served as a mine of fable for sculptors and for the Attic dramatists.

27. **Sportive 'Homeric' Pieces.** Some humorous trifles went under 'Homer's' name, merely because they were in the epic style of Ionia. Two were celebrated. *Margîtes* ('The Booby') was a comic poem on a silly jack-of-all-trades, half milksop, half coxcomb, 'who knew many things, but knew them all badly.' We have only a few verses of the piece, which may have been as old as about 700 B.C., and which Aristotle regards as the first germ of comedy. The *Battle of the Frogs and Mice* (*Batrachomyomachia*), of which we have about 300 lines, was sometimes ascribed to Pigres, brother of Artemisia, the queen of Halicarnassus who distinguished herself in Xerxes' army. But it more probably belongs to the declining days of the literature, and some put it as late as 160 B.C. It was one of the first and most popular *parodies* in the old world.

28. **Hesiod.** Besides Homer, another great poet was named in Greek tradition as the founder of an epic school. This was Hesiod. What is known of his life is gathered chiefly from the poems ascribed to him. His father Dius had come from Cymê, a town of Aeolis in Asia Minor, to the old home of the Aeolians in Greece Proper, and had settled on an upland farm at the village of Ascra, near Mount Helicon in Boeotia. Poverty is said to have been his reason. He found, perhaps, that he could not make his way in the busy commercial world of Asia Minor, and resolved to retire to a quiet farmer's life in the old country,

where at least a subsistence was secure. Hesiod grumbles that Ascra was 'dreary in winter, sultry in summer, good at no season,' but he seems to be unjust to the fertile and well-watered region. Here he fed his father's sheep on Mount Helicon, and began his work as poet. Later in life he is said to have removed to Naupactus on the Gulf of Corinth in Locris—thus passing from Aeolian to Dorian surroundings; and the Dorian influence has left traces in his work. He was murdered (the legend said) at Oenoe in Locris, and buried at Naupactus, whence his remains were transferred in later times to the Boeotian Orchornenus.

His date cannot be exactly fixed. It is certain, that he must be later, by some 80 or 100 years than that great time of Ionian epos which is represented by the *Iliad.* On the other hand, he must be considerably earlier than those poets of the 7th century B.C. who stand in the dawning light of history. This seems clear, not only from particular facts, but also from the way in which Hesiod is mentioned by Greek writers. Homer and Hesiod are the two names that are always joined by Greek tradition as representing the very oldest poetry. No third name, which we can connect with authentic work, is so decisively thrown back by Greek belief into a far past. The best ancient and modern authorities are probably right in placing Hesiod about 850—800 B.C.

29. **The Homeric and Hesiodic types of Epic Poetry.** Hesiod has told us how he came to be a poet. He was feeding his sheep on Mount Helicon when the Muses appeared to him. 'Houseless shepherds!' they cried, speaking to Hesiod as the representative shepherd—'Creatures of reproach, natures gross! We can say many things that are false, though like truth; but we know also when we choose, *how to utter true things.*' And then they commission Hesiod to be their spokesman. This strikes the keynote of Hesiod's poetry. Its task was *to utter true things*. The Homeric poetry of Ionia moves among visions of the heroic past, to which the poet's art gives an ideal glory. The Hesiodic

poetry of Boeotia moves among realities. It deals with the tasks of daily life, with the practical duty of man, and with those *facts* about gods and heroes which make up religious knowledge.

30. The life out of which Hesiod's poetry sprang was very different from that of Ionia. The daily routine of dwellers in Boeotia was that of a quiet, inland farming life; it was not varied by brisk commerce or seafaring adventure, by the bustle of an Ionian harbour when a ship came in from Sidon or the Nile, by the visits of men wearing a strange garb and speaking in broken Greek of the marvels of strange lands, or listening while, amid an eager crowd, some Ionian minstrel chanted in the market-place a lay of that great war in which Achilles and Hector fought. The farmer in the old country led a life much less stirring to the imagination. How could he best use the winter and spring, so as to earn his rest in summer when artichokes ripen and the cicala sings, when fat kids and temperate cups refresh the sun-scorched toiler? When should he begin to reap his corn? How should the axle-tree of a waggon be made, and what is the best wood for a plough-tail or a pole? How are the cattle to be kept fit for work? What is the best way of drying grapes? And last, not least, what are the lucky or unlucky days of the month for doing all these things ? These were the questions in Boeotia.

31. But Hesiod's poetry was not addressed merely to rural labourers: it spoke to the nobles just as much,—it spoke to all men, setting forth the *moral precepts* and the *religious lore* which the poet thought most important for them to know. The worship of Apollo at **Delphi** had already spread its influence through Greece Proper, and, under the teaching of the Delphic priesthood, carried with it a belief in the immortality of the soul. This belief was also inculcated by the Dorian priesthoods of the Peloponnesus, who traced their mystic doctrine from the mythical Melampus, a seer of Argos. One of the chief points in this doctrine was the existence of *daemonic* beings, intermediate between gods and men, and connecting living men with the

dead. We see that Hesiod's poetry had some contact with this Dorian teaching. He speaks of departed men of the golden Age becoming *spirits* (*daimones*), and haunting the earth, invisible, to watch over justice. We see too, how, in the spirit of Delphi, he regards the office of the *poet* as closely connected with the office of the *prophet,* and speaks as if he had some authority from the gods to proclaim what men ought to believe and do.

32. **Hesiod's Works and Days.** Hesiod's chief poem is called 'Works and Days,' because it treats of the works which the farmer has to do, and of the days which are lucky or unlucky for doing them. The name of **didactic** or *teaching* poetry is properly given to poetry which puts the facts of some art or science into verse, and surrounds them with beauties of imagination or sentiment. Hesiod's poem is the earliest extant poem of this sort. But we must distinguish Hesiod's work from that of later 'didactic' authors who chose verse instead of prose merely because it pleased their taste, or who merely put into verse what had already been said in prose. In Hesiod's time there was no prose literature, and if he wanted to get a public hearing for his thoughts he was obliged to put them into verse. His object was to supply a practical need. His poem ought not to be classed with an exquisite work of literary art, such as Virgil's *Georgics,* but rather with such a work as that of Thomas Tusser, a Suffolk farmer in the 16th century, who wrote his 'Five Hundred Points of Good Husbandry' in homely verse, to help other farmers.

33. In the *Works and Days* there are really three parts, which may once have been distinct—an introductory poem addressed to his brother Perses,—then the 'Works' proper,—and then the 'Days' or Calendar. Hesiod and his younger brother Perses had divided the property left by their father, but Perses had got the larger share, Hesiod says, by bribing certain judges. Perses now lived in luxurious idleness, and presently threatened Hesiod with another lawsuit. Hesiod reminds Perses and the corrupt judges that *Justice,* when wronged on earth, takes refuge with

her father Zeus. Here we meet with the earliest *fable* in Greek literature, the *Hawk and the Nightingale.* The hawk has the nightingale in his clutches, and in answer to the captive's complaint reminds her that 'might is right.' Here, too, the poet describes the *Five Ages* of the world—the age of gold, of silver, of bronze, of heroes or demi-gods (put in, apparently, to make a place for the Homeric heroes)—and of iron, in which the poet himself has the misfortune to live. From *justice* the theme changes to *work.* '*Work,* foolish Perses, *work the work that the gods have set for men!*' A man who means to work should provide himself with a house, an ox and household stuff, and that speedily, for delay fills no granaries. The cry of the crane is the signal for ploughing: the master must guide the plough, with many a prayer to Zeus and Demeter, while a slave follows and covers up the seed, 'to give trouble to the birds.' Then come the rules for all the works and seasons of the farmer's year,—and lastly the Calendar, the list of lucky or unlucky days. 'Sometimes a day is a stepmother, sometimes a mother; therefore blessed is he who knows them all, and works his work unblamed by the immortals.'

34. The **Theogony** or *Origin of the Gods,* a poem of 1022 lines, has come to us in a confused and corrupt state, but is probably Hesiod's in the main, as the ancients generally held. The belief that the world was *created* by a Supreme Power, though very old and widely-spread in the East, was never congenial to the Greeks. Their tendency was to think of the world, not as *made* by a Creator, but as *born* out of pre-existing elements. They spoke of the gods as 'living for ever,' but they did not believe that the gods had lived from eternity. So Hesiod's *Theogony* falls into two chief parts. The first part tells how the visible order of Nature arose. The second tells how the gods were born.

From Chaos, a confused mass of atoms, come forth Earth, Tartarus (Hell), Eros (Love), and Erebos (Night). Erebos brings forth Aether (Day). Earth produces the Heaven and the Sea. The ruling idea of the legend is that light grows out of darkness and form out of formlessness.

Earth, and her own offspring Heaven, now become the parents of superhuman beings in the human form, namely the elder gods and the gigantic Titans. Cronus, one of these elder gods, begets Zeus. Zeus makes war on his father Cronus, who is helped by the Titans, and overthrows him. Zeus thus becomes king of the Olympian gods, whose descent is next traced. Here the original poem perhaps ended. In our text the last 80 lines commence a genealogy of *Heroes*, sons born by goddesses to men.

35. **Source and Influence of the Theogony.** The poet's chief sources in the *Theogony* must have been old hymns preserved in the temples, and folklore which lived in the mouths of the people. He was not making a new system on an artistic plan of his own. He was simply trying to piece together a very old system of which he had found the fragments, and which he did not always understand. The legends massed together, rather than blended, in this poem carry us back to days when the Greek imagination was still struggling to bring clear shapes out of the grand, but wild and half formless, legends of an Asiatic Nature-worship. Hesiod's *Theogony* was always a standard authority for Greeks who wrote or taught about the gods. But it would be misleading to compare its popular influence to that of the Sacred Books of India or Persia. The Greeks never had anything really like these, just as they never had a sacerdotal caste, though there were priests of local worships and temples. The Greek mind was sometimes drawn towards mystic doctrine, but through its whole history it resisted the rule of priests.

36. **The Shield of Heracles,** not by Hesiod, but of later and perhaps composite authorship, is an epic lay in 480 lines, and has for its framework a fight between Heracles—son of Zeus, and the strongest of mortals—and Cycnus, son of the War-god Ares. Cycnus was a robber who used to plunder pilgrims on their way through Thessaly to the temple of Apollo at Delphi.

This fight takes place in the sacred precinct of Apollo at Pagasae in Thessaly. Heracles slays Cycnus, but the robber's father, the god Ares, escapes to Olympus. The fight, however, is a mere pretext for describing the shield made for Heracles by the god Hephaestus. The description is imitated from that of the shield of Achilles in the 18th Book of the Iliad, but is greatly inferior to it. The Homeric poet draws mainly on his own fancy. The Hesiodic poet draws from real works of art, and dramatises them. Heracles has the armour of an ordinary warrior; but as early as 648 B.C. the epic poet Peisander set the example of equipping Heracles with the lion's skin, club, and bow.[3] Short epic pieces of this kind were often copied by the early lyric poets. This piece belongs to the decline of the Hesiodic school, when it was beginning to lose its distinctness from the Ionian school of Homer. Some rhapsodist has enlarged it, by prefixing to it 56 lines belonging to another poem which bore Hesiod's name—the *Eoiae*, or *Catalogue of Heroic Women.*

37. This poem, the Eoiae (so called because each new personage was introduced by the words *ê hoiê*, 'or such as was she,') celebrated the heroines of Boeotia and Thessaly from whose union with gods had sprung heroes; and formed a fourth book to the *Catalogue of Women*, an epic history of Dorian and Aeolian women, famous indeed, but not of that half-divine rank which belonged to the 'heroines.' These names of poems show how the Hesiodic school was connected with Dorian Locris, where the position of women was peculiarly high. Such poems, whoever wrote them, carried on Hesiod's idea—**to gather up the old legends**, as they lived on in Greece Proper—treating them, not as the Ionian poets did, ideally, but rather as **relics of a sacred history**. The *Aegimius* celebrated a Dorian king who made war against the Lapithae, and who was a friend of Heracles,—as was *Ceyx*, king of Trachis, whose marriage was the subject of another poem. These two poems, and the *Shield of Heracles*, show us that Heracles, an especially Dorian hero, was a favourite with the Hesiodic poets. The titles of two other lost poems—the *Maxims of Cheiron*, the wise Centaur, and the *Lay*

of Melampus, a record of prophets and prophetic lore—bring out the moral and mystic sides of the school.

38. The point at which the Homeric and the Hesiodic schools begin to meet is found, for us, in the **Homeric Hymns**. A collection of thirty-three longer or shorter pieces in hexameter verse has come down to us with the title, 'Hymns or Preludes of Homer and the Homeridae.' To the title of 'Hymns' they have no strict claim. They have nothing to do with the formal worship of the gods. It was usual for a rhapsodist to preface the recitation of epic poetry by an address to some god. If he was reciting at a festival, this prefatory address would be, of course, to the god of the festival. Or he might choose to honour some favourite local deity. Otherwise his choice of a deity was free. Pindar speaks of '*a prelude to Zeus*,' '*from which the Homerid bards* (*i.e.* the rhapsodists) *oft draw out their linked song.*' Our 'Homeric Hymns' are simply a collection of such preludes—some long, some short—to various deities, drawn up, probably in Attica, for the use of rhapsodists. Two-thirds of the thirty-three end with a verse in which the singer says that now he will pass from the god to another theme. And two of them say expressly that this theme is to be the praise of heroes. One of them (No. 8, a short prayer to Ares) is distinct from the rest in character and tone. All the rest are epic in spirit. Most of them narrate some passage in the life of the deity addressed. The style is that of the Ionian or 'Homeric' school. But the Boeotian and Dorian, or 'Hesiodic' school, can be clearly traced in some places, as in the Hymn to the Pythian Apollo (No. 1, from v. 178 to the end), the Hymn to Pan (No. 19), and the address to Apollo and the Muses (No. 25). Hardly two of the whole collection, probably, are by the same hand. Not one of them belongs to the best days of Ionian epic poetry. The period from 750 to 500 B.C. marks roughly the limits of their origin, though the hymn to Hermes may be later; but few can be older than 660 B.C.

39. **The Five Greater Hymns.** The first 'Hymn' of our collection is made up of two distinct preludes: one to the DELIAN

APOLLO (verses 1 to 177); and one to the PYTHIAN APOLLO (v. 178 to the end). The first tells us how Apollo was born in Delos and how his great festival was established there. The second tells how Apollo came down from Olympus to seek a shrine on earth, and after many wanderings reached Delphi, where his temple and priesthood were founded. HERMES (Hymn II), the young god of guile, steals the cattle of Apollo from the Pierian hills, and transfers them to his own pastures of Arcadia. APHRODITE (Hymn III), the goddess of beauty, appears to Anchises, a young Trojan prince, as he watches his flocks on Mount Ida; and, before she re-ascends to Olympus, unfolds the great destiny that awaits their son Aeneas. DEMETER (Hymn IV), in search for Persephone, whom Pluto has carried away to the shades, visits Eleusis, and there founds her worship, and recovers her daughter.

40. **The Ionian Festival at Delos.** The Hymn to the Delian Apollo gives us a glimpse of the bright morning-time of Ionian song—the spring festival of Apollo at Delos,—a sort of fair as well,—to which Ionians came from the coast of Asia Minor and from the islands of the Aegean. 'There, in thy honour, Apollo, the long-robed Ionians assemble, with their children and their gracious dames. So often as they hold thy festival, they celebrate thee, for thy joy, with boxing and dancing and song. A man would say that they were strangers to death and old age evermore, who should come on the Ionians thus gathered; for he would see the goodliness of all the people, and would rejoice in his soul, beholding the men and the fairly-cinctured women, and their swift ships and their great wealth; and besides, that wonder of which the fame shall not perish, the maidens of Delos, handmaidens of Apollo the Far-Darter. First they hymn Apollo, then Leto and Artemis delighting in arrows; and then they sing the praise of heroes of yore and of women, and throw their spell over the tribes of men.' But even, perhaps, when this song was first sung, the time had come when Ionian minstrels should not sing only the lays of the heroic past. As men's life became larger and more thoughtful, as freedom and knowledge

grew, these Ionian worshippers at Delos learned to welcome the first tones of a new poetry, busied with the joys and sorrows of the living.

Notes

1. According to one interpretation of the doubtful tradition, Solon provided that Homeric recitations should follow an authorised text (*hypobolê*); Hipparchus, that they should observe a regular order (*hypolêpsis*). Others take *hypobolê* to mean 'prompting,'—giving the cue.

2. *Homerus* means 'fitted together,' not 'fitting together'; and it is doubtful whether it can be explained to mean 'versifier' or 'compiler.'

3. An inscribed vase, of the date 450—400 B.C., found at Rhodes, has for one of its subjects the slaying of Cycnus by Heracles. Mr Percy Gardner thinks that the artist of this vase probably had before him those parts of the Hesiodic poem which describe the arming of Heracles and the fight, but not that part which describes the shield. (*Journal of Philology*, vol. VII, p. 215, 1877.)

3

ELEGIAC AND IAMBIC POETRY—LYRIC POETRY

I. **Elegiac and Iambic Poetry, 700—500** B.C.: Callînus (E.), 690 B.C.; Tyrtaeus (E.), 675; Archilochus (E. and I.), 670; Simonides of Amorgus (I.), 660; Mimnermus (E.), 620; Solon (E. and I.), 594; Theognis (E.), 540; Phocylides (E.), 540; Xenophanes (E.), 510; Hippônax (I.), 540; Simonides of Ceos (E.), 480.

II. **Lyric Poetry, 670—440** B.C. 1. *Aeolian School*: Alcaeus, Sappho, 610 B.C. Anacreon, 530. 2. *Dorian School*: Alcman, 660 B.C.; Stesichorus, 620; Arion, 600 B.C.; Ibycus, 540 B.C. 3. *Lyric Poetry, Dorian in form, but national in spirit*: Simonides of Ceos, 480 B.C.; Pindar, 470.

1. **Rise of the New Poetry.** Between 750 and 500 B.C. a great change passed over the Greek world. Monarchy gave place to oligarchy, (the rule of the noble few), and this again, in many places, to a tyranny,—*i.e.* the unconstitutional rule of one man who had seized supreme power. Lastly, as the tyrannies were put down, democracies arose in many cities, especially among the Ionians. These revolutions brought much strife with them; men's minds were moved and their experiences enlarged. The ordinary Homeric man is merely one of a crowd, who is sometimes asked to say Yes or No. Now the private citizen begins to think and act more independently. He has wider influence, higher work, finer pleasures, more to stir his mind and warm his fancy. Knowledge is widening its circle, the fine arts are slowly ripening, science is struggling to its birth, life is

growing eager and full. But as yet there is hardly any prose writing. If a man would get a hearing for his thoughts, he must utter them in verse. We have seen how *reflection* has been gradually coming into poetry. The *Iliad* has little of it; the *Odyssey*, more; Hesiod much more. And now, about 700 B.C., in this dawn of large promise, the poet comes forward with his first distinct attempt to interest other people in his own thoughts and feelings. The expression took two forms, created almost at the same time—those of *Elegiac* and *Iambic* poetry.

2. **Elegiac Metre.** The word *elegos* is probably not Greek by origin, but the Greek form of a name given by the Carians and Lydians of Asia Minor to a mournful song accompanied by the flute. A particular metre, being at first used by the Greeks for such a song, may thence have come to be called the elegiac metre. This was borrowed from the familiar and universal metre of the earliest Greek poetry,— the epic hexameter. Take these two hexameters of Clough's:

1 2 3 4 5
O let us | try, he | answered, the | waters them | selves
6
will sup | port us, |
1 2 3 4 5
Yea very | ripples and | waves will | form to a | boat
6
under | neath us.

In the second line, omit *will* from the 3rd place and *us* from the 6th. It has now been turned from an hexameter, or 'six-metre' verse, into a pentameter, or 'five-metre' verse, since the two odd syllables, 'waves' and 'neath,' count together as one metre. And the two lines together now form an *elegiac couplet*. A poem composed of such couplets is an elegiac poem.

3. **Character of Elegiac Poetry.** 'Elegy,' Coleridge says, 'is the form of poetry natural to the reflective mind;' and it may treat of any subject, he adds, if it does so with reference to the poet himself. Greek elegy exemplifies this. It deals with the greatest variety of subjects,—the wars which the poet's city is

waging,—the political feuds among the citizens,—the laws or principles which the poet wishes them to adopt,—his own opinions on the manners or morals of the day,—his views as to the best way of enjoying life,—festive pleasure,—lamentation for the dead,— everything that the poet and his friends are wont to think or talk of. But, whatever the subject may be, this early Greek Elegy has always two general characteristics. It is the expression of the poet's own thoughts or feelings, addressed to a sympathising society. And this expression, though free and full, though animated or earnest, stops short of being passionate. The later Greek poets of the Alexandrian age wrote elaborate love-elegies of a languishing kind, or made elegy a vehicle for the display of learning. The Roman elegiac poets imitated chiefly this Alexandrian type, and, with all their beauty, have little of the fresh, simple animation or pathos that belonged to the elegiac poetry of early Greece.

4. The flute-accompaniment was an essential part of early Greek elegies, which were sung after dinner among friends, and had a social, almost confidential, and often convivial character. This soft music of the *Lydian* flute must be distinguished from those wild, stirring strains of the *Phrygian* flute which belonged to the worship of Cybele. The connexion with the flute points to the non-Greek origin of Elegy. The musical instruments specially developed by the Greeks themselves were string-instruments; wind-instruments, such as the flute, came to them from their neighbours in Asia.

5. **Iambic Poetry.** 'Iambus' (◡–) is probably a Greek word, from *iapto,* 'to dart or shoot,' hence 'a taunt or gibe,' because the light, smart iambic metre was first used in the *raillery* which entered into the worship of Demeter, as into a modern carnival. The story, invented to explain this usage, was that, when Demeter was plunged in grief for the loss of her daughter, the first smile was drawn from her by the jests of the maiden Iambê. The commonest form of the iambic metre was the verse of six iambic feet or three iambic metres (hence 'iambic trimeter') in

which the dialogue of Attic tragedy was written. Shakespeare often uses it in rapid dialogue or retort; here is an iambic trimeter:

Then lét's | make háste | awáy, || and loók | untó | the máin.

This metre, at first used for satire, was fitted to express *any pointed thought.* Thus it was used for *fables*, and for reflection of a graver, keener sort than suited elegy. It was the form in which the more original and intense spirits loved to utter their scorn or their deeper thought and emotion. The elegiac and early iambic poetry, both Ionian, may be considered as forming together a single stage in the growth of the literature, between the epic and the lyric.

6. **Callînus** of Ephesus, about 690 B.C., is the earliest of the Greek Elegists. During the reign of Ardys, King of Lydia, the Cimmerians, a fierce tribe of northern Europe, broke into Asia Minor, took Sardis, and invaded Ionia. Another horde, the Trêres, followed them, but were driven back. The Cimmerians, however, long vexed Ionia; and the verses of Callînus which remain are a spirited appeal to the Ionians to rise against the invaders. The music of the flute, martial as well as funereal, easily lent itself to warlike elegy.

7. **Tyrtaeus** lived in the days of the Second Messenian War (685—668 B.C.), and was an Ionian, if not actually a native of Attica, who migrated to Lacedaemon. In a poem called *Good Government* (Eunomia) he sought to allay a sedition among the Spartans—those whose estates had been ravaged in the war were clamouring for a new distribution of lands—by reminding them that the Spartan laws have been founded by Apollo himself. The two Kings, the Elders and the Commons together form a body to which each member owes loyalty. In a series of stirring elegiac lays, called his *Exhortations,* he urged the Spartans to fight to the death against the Messenians. In after-days the Spartans used to recite these Spartan songs of an Ionian bard at the evening camp-meal. Tyrtaeus wrote marching-songs too,

which the Spartans sang as they went into battle—not elegiac, but in an *anapaestic* metre (◡◡–): one of them begins,

To the frónt, | ye brave sóns | of Spárta.

8. **Archilochus** (670 B.C.), an Ionian of the isle of Paros, who migrated to the isle of Thasos with a colony, was a vigorous genius, whom the Greeks of the classical age even ranked with Homer and Pindar and Sophocles as one of the great original forces in their literature. The islanders of Thasos were often at war with the Thracians of the mainland, and Archilochus, a warrior himself, sang of war in his elegies. He turned elegy also to the mourning for the dead, in a beautiful poem on his sister's husband, who was drowned at sea. But his native power came out most in the mastery which he showed over *iambic* poetry, first made famous by his skill. The story that his iambic satire drove Neobulê and her sisters to suicide (the father Lycambes had promised Neobulê in marriage to Archilochus, and had broken his word) may be a myth, but assuredly it expresses the terrible power of this new scourge, public satire, over the hot Ionian blood. **Simonides of Amorgus** (660 B.C.) carried on the satiric use of iambic poetry, but in a general, rather than a personal, form. The longest fragment is a quaint satire on the female sex, in which it is said that the gods have made women after the natures of various animals—the fox, the cat, and so forth.

9. **Mimnermus** (620 B.C.) of Smyrna makes his elegiac poetry a true mirror of soft, degenerate Ionia. He looks back sorrowfully to the old days when the men of Smyrna drove back the Lydians: but he acquiesces. Life, he says, is worthless when its prime is over: 'may the doom of death overtake me, free from disease and care,—at sixty.' He pities the very sun for his daily labour in lighting the world.

Solon (594 B.C.), the great lawgiver, used elegy more in the manner of Callînus or Tyrtaeus. In his early manhood, his stirring verses moved the Athenians to win back Salamis from the Megarians. And when he had carried his great reforms, elegy became the voice of his calm joy. 'I gave the common folk as much strength as is enough, neither less nor more than their due meed; but as to those who had rule, and the splendour of wealth, to them also I gave counsel, even that they should not uphold cruelty. I took my stand, I spread my strong shield over both, and suffered neither to prevail by wrong.' Solon raised the dignity of Elegy by thus confiding to it his great political deeds; and he made it also the vehicle of *moral* teaching. His use of *iambic* poetry shows the old tradition, for in it he brings out the controversial side of his public life.

10. **Theognis** (540 B.C.), a Dorian noble of Megara, has left us about 1400 elegiac verses in the Ionic dialect—much more than we have from any early Greek elegist—in which he seeks to impress the orthodox doctrines of the Dorian aristocracy on a young Megarian noble named Cyrnus, and puts in many quaint bits of worldly wisdom by the way. His tone, and the respectability of his views, made him a standard author in Attic schools, and his text has been much confused by additions. He was driven out of Megara by a democratic revolution, and visited the vine-clad lowlands of Euboea, and then Sicily—returning to Megara at last, for he seems to have been there shortly before the Persian Wars. He speaks regretfully of a time when the common folk of Megara were clad in goatskins, and were as shy of the city as deer—keeping to the hills or the seashore. The nobles are the *good,* the people are 'poor creatures.' 'Money,' he says, 'mixes race'; but such marriages are the bane of the city. Conservative Attic fathers liked his politics; and his wise sayings were so well-known that it became a proverb, *I knew that before Theognis was born.*

11. **Phocylides** of Miletus (540 B.C.) was another moralising elegist, whose short pithy precepts were very popular in Greece. He also wrote hexameters, of which we have a few; but the poem in 230 verses, entitled 'Maxims,' under his name, is probably by an Alexandrian Jew of the first century A.D. **Xenophanes** of Colophon (510 B.C.), founder of the Eleatic

philosophy, made elegy the utterance of philosophic thought. He blamed Homer and Hesiod for imputing immoral acts to the gods, and said that it would be better to record good deeds that had really been done than fables about Titans and Centaurs. Poetry was the great popular influence in early Greece, and we often find Greek philosophy trying to correct this influence. Xenophanes is interesting as a poet-philosopher protesting against the vulgar poetry.

Simonides of Ceos (480 B.C.) wrote beautiful elegiac epitaphs on Greeks who fell in the Persian Wars; but he was more famous as a lyric poet. In the Attic age (475—300 B.C.), when dramatic poetry was foremost, the elegiac was still popular as an easy, elegant form of composition which all cultivated men could use on occasion—as for inscriptions, epigrams, or short pieces meant for friends. We hear of elegiacs having been written not only by all the great Attic poets, but by the Attic masters of prose, such as Thucydides, Plato, Aristotle, Demosthenes. In the Alexandrian age, sentiment, court flattery, learning, all found elegiac expression.

12. **Hipponax** of Ephesus (540 B.C.) was driven from his native city and reduced to poverty by its tyrants, and settled at Clazomenae. He was an ugly, spiteful little man, and two sculptors of the place caricatured him; whereupon he revenged himself in bitter iambic verses, composed in a curious hobbling metre, produced by changing the last foot (◡·–) into a spondee (– —). This metre became known as the 'lame' or 'limping' iambic ('choliambic': 'scazon'). The fragments have some interest as giving us glimpses of the lower Ionian life, and some homely words. *Fables* found a natural expression in iambic verse — especially *beast-fables*, which have always something of satire in them ; thus an iambic fragment of Archilochus begins a fable about an alliance between a fox and an eagle. The Alexandrian poet CALLIMACHUS used the 'limping' iambic metre of Hippônax, and it was adopted also by BABRIUS (about 40 A.D.) in his collection of fables.

13. **Lyric Poetry,** in the usual modern sense, is such poetry as is capable by its form of being sung to music. The Greek lyric poetry was not only capable of being sung to music, but was inseparable from music. **The poetry and the music together formed a single work of art.** All the Greek lyric poets were necessarily, in some degree, musical composers. 'Lyric' was not the usual Greek word. The Greeks more commonly spoke of **melic** poetry, *i.e.* poetry meant to be *sung,* as distinguished from poetry meant, like the epic, to be *recited.*

14. It follows that Greek lyric poetry could not be artistic until the art of **Music** had been developed. TERPANDER (about 660 B.C.) is said to have made the first great epoch in Greek music by giving the lyre seven strings instead of four. This means the discovery of the octave; for, as the 8th note only reproduces the Ist, an instrument with seven notes can express the whole diatonic scale. Henceforth the Greeks distinguished three principal **modes** or 'harmonies' with four subordinate modes; the seven-stringed instrument could be tuned to any one of these seven 'modes.' The distinction between the 'modes' corresponded to our distinction between 'major' and 'minor' keys. The difference of the 'modes' depended on the place of the semitones in the octave. The **Dorian mode** (a minor scale, as we should say) was thought appropriate to earnest or to warlike melodies; the **Phrygian** (also of a minor character) to passion; the **Lydian** (a major scale) to soft pathos. The Greeks had a subtle feeling for the moral tone of the 'modes.' Plato would admit the lofty Phrygian and the spirited Dorian modes in his ideal commonwealth, but not the enervating Lydian. The little that is known of Greek melody suggests that it was simple, but not, to our ears, especially pleasing. It is likely that they knew some of the main principles of harmony; but their practice, at least, seems to have been somewhat crude.

15. Greek lyric poetry was not limited to a small circle by being thus inseparable from music, for **music was a regular part of a liberal education**. Boys at school had lessons from the

harpist, and learned at least to distinguish the different 'modes,' and to be able to play a simple accompaniment. In one of the comedies of Aristophanes it is a joke against the demagogue Cleon that when he was a boy at school he always insisted on tuning his lyre on the Dorian scale (with a pun on *dôron,* 'a bribe'), and could never learn any other, till the music-master lost all patience. Aristotle insists on the value of this practical training in music, not only as a discipline of taste and character, but as preparing a noble source of recreation for after life; he only urges that a citizen must not unfit himself for manly exercises in labouring to become as skilful as a professional musician.

16. **Aeolian Lyric Poetry.** The Aeolians of **Lesbos** were famous from early times for music and lyric song, regularly cultivated in their musical schools. The old legend told how, when the bard Orpheus was torn in pieces by the bacchants of Thrace, his head and his lyre were swept down the river Hebrus to the sea, while song still came from the dead lips, and were washed ashore at Antissa in Lesbos, where the Lesbians buried the head, and hung up the lyre in the temple of Apollo. Both the early poetry of Pieria and the soft instrumental music of Lydia had influenced the lyric art of Lesbos. Here the fiery Aeolian temperament was quickened by special causes. In the 7th century B.C. Lesbos was a commercial and naval power. Party strife was restless in the island. The nobles, whose power was not seldom threatened or overthrown by the commons, lived a life of stormy excitement, of love and war, of luxury and hardship, of haughty dominion or homeless exile.

These changes, like sunlight and shadow flitting over a summer sea, were mirrored in their Lyric Poetry. It had a rapid flow, a gay careless grace often lit up by a sudden glow of passion, and a wonderful melody. But the Aeolian dialect was comparatively meagre and rude for the uses of art; and this prevented the Aeolian poetry from ever becoming so generally popular as the Dorian. The Aeolian ode was usually meant to be sung by a single voice, and was on a light and simple plan, suited to the swift and burning utterance of the poet's mood.

17. **Alcaeus**, a Lesbian noble of Mitylene (about 611—580 B.C.), took an active part in the strife of the Lesbian nobles against the commons, as well as in a war between Lesbos and Athens for the possession of Sigeum in the Troad: and he told in his poetry—with the same frankness as Archilochus and Horace—how he once threw away his shield. About 606 B.C., when Pittacus was made dictator of Lesbos by the commons, Alcaeus with his two brothers went into exile, and spent many years in the East. He was finally reconciled to the home government, and died in Lesbos. He wrote hymns to the gods, political songs, drinking songs, songs of war and love; but we have only a few fragments of his poetry. One fragment describes a warrior's hall hung round with gleaming, white-plumed helmets, greaves, cuirasses, shields and broadswords. Another compares the Lesbian State to a storm-tossed ship; the water is coming in, the sail is torn, the anchor will not hold, the waves come this way and that,—the mariners are driven before the tempest. This, like some others, is in that *Alcaic* stanza which takes its name from him, and which Horace adopted. Mr Tennyson has given a specimen of it to English readers:

O mighty-mouthed inventor of harmonies,
O skilled to sing of time or eternity,
God-gifted organ-voice of England,
Milton, a name to resound for ages.

In another fragment Alcaeus bids his comrades forget the wild weather outside the warm room, heap logs on the fire, mix the dark wine, and call for garlands and perfumes. Elsewhere he denounces the tyrants of Lesbos. Alcaeus was in some respects not unlike a Royalist soldier of the age of the Stuarts. He had the high spirit and reckless gaiety, the love of country bound up with belief in a caste, the licence tempered by generosity and sometimes by tenderness, of a cavalier who has seen good and evil days. Two lines of his remain to link his name with another not less famous. 'Chaste Sappho, with thy dark tresses and thy gentle smile, fain would I speak, but awe restrains me.'

18. **Sappho** (610 B.C.) was a woman of surpassing artistic genius, exquisitely sensitive to the harmonies of form and sound, whose passionate energy found a natural expression in poetry, and who uttered in poetry her worship of beauty. No Greek woman of the Ionian race is known to have excelled in poetry; and no Aeolian or Dorian woman, except Sappho, is known to have made poetry the personal expression of an intense life. She was helped to do this, not only by the glow of the Aeolian blood that fired her genius, but also by the large and rich life with which Aeolian society surrounded women of the higher rank. This is what gives their unique interest to the few fragments that remain of her work, fragments of incomparable melody, with a clear flame burning through the musical words. She appears to have been the centre of a poetical school or group, and from one of the most celebrated of her disciples, ERINNA, some fragments remain. Sappho is said to have left Mitylene about 596 B.C., and to have died in Sicily. The story of her hopeless love for Phaon, and of her springing from the Leucadian cliff into the sea, is probably a later fable. The *Sapphic* stanza was only one of many metres used by Sappho. Horace, in adapting it for Latin use, has modified its rules, and retains its most characteristic rhythm only in a few lines, such as *Laurea donandus Apollinari*. The following stanza preserves the genuine Greek cadence:

> Faded every violet, all the roses;
> Gone the glorious promise, and the victim
> Broken in this anger of Aphrodite
> Yields to the victor.[1]

19. **Anacreon,** of Teos, a city on the coast of Ionia, who flourished, about 530 B.C., wrote in a mainly Ionian dialect, but is akin to the Aeolian School in the matter and the form of his lyrics. He lived for some time at the brilliant court of Polycrates,

tyrant of Samos; then at Athens with Hipparchus, son of the tyrant Peisistratus, and afterwards, it is said, in Thessaly with the princely Aleuadae. Anacreon was the poet of pleasure. His pliant Ionian nature fitted him for the life of a gay society. Love, wine, and music were his joys. He seems to have gone through his long life on easy terms with the world, cherishing no ambition except that of enjoyment, and no regret save for the flight of youth. The few genuine fragments of his work are from hymns, or poems of love and society; they show a pure style, light grace, sweetness, and touches of satirical humour. The collection of about 60 short pieces under his name was first put together in the tenth century. These spurious *Anacreontea* are probably all of the Christian era, and many as late as 500 A.D. They have, on the whole, little of classical merit; the form is somewhat wooden, and the fancy barren; but they are often as bright and pretty as elegant industry could make them.

20. **Dorian Lyric Poetry.** Dorian and Aeolian life had this in common, that both were based on the rule of a warlike aristocracy. But the Aeolian State was frequently shaken by fickle and fiery passion: it was indeed the storm-driven ship to which Alcaeus likened it. The Dorian State was anchored to the steadfast faith of the Dorian people in their gods and in the usages handed down by their fathers. A Dorian commonwealth was a compact body held together by a military discipline, to which each member was proudly loyal. A stamp, of severe symmetry and majesty belonged to the rites of the Dorian religion, to the Dorian temples and statues and poems. Dorian Lyric Poetry was the expression of Dorian life in all its public or social energies. The Dorian lyrist, unlike the Aeolian, says little of himself. He sets forth the consecrated tradition and the ancestral glory of the Dorian race for Dorians gathered at the worship of the gods, at the celebration of some victory in the athletic games, at a festival commemorating the foundation of a city or the great deeds of a living king. In its most distinctive forms, Dorian Lyric Poetry was meant to be sung, not by a single voice, but by a **chorus**.

21. It follows from the nature of this poetry that its history does not present to us a single personality so strongly marked as those of the Aeolian Alcaeus and Sappho. We have here, not vivid characters, but rather phases in the development of an art. **Alcman** of Sparta (660 B.C.) wrote hymns; songs to be sung during processions to temples (*prosodia*), especially *parthenia* to be sung by maidens; paeans, *i.e.* songs imploring or praising the health-giving power of the gods; nuptial chants, and love-songs. He was the first who gave an artistic form to the **choral** lyric by arranging that the chorus, while singing, should execute alternately a movement to the right (*strophê,* 'turning'), and a movement to the left (*antistrophê*); and he composed the songs which the chorus was to sing in couples of stanzas called **strophê** and **antistrophê**, answering to these balanced movements. His fragments have a special interest as samples of the Dorian dialect in its Laconian or Spartan variety.

22. **Stesichorus** of Himera in Sicily (620 B.C.)—whose real name was Tisias, but whose skill procured him this name Stesichorus, 'marshal of choruses,'—completed the form of the choral lyric by adding to *strophê* and *antistrophê* a third part, the **epôde**, sung by the chorus while it remained stationary after the movements to right and left. Stesichorus treated *epic* subjects, such as the legends of Troy, in his lyric poems; hence Horace speaks of his *stately* muse. There was a story current in the old world that Helen, now a goddess, struck this poet blind because he had sung evil of her, but restored his sight when he had composed a recantation (or *palinode*) beginning : 'This story is not true; thou didst *not* go to Troy.'

23. **Arion,** (600 B.C.), though a Lesbian by birth belongs by art rather to the Dorian school. His great work was to give the **dithyramb**, or choral hymn to Dionysus, a finished choral form, by fixing the number (50) of the *cyclic* or circular chorus that was to sing it, grouped round the altar, and by dividing the singing and acting parts clearly from each other. We have a fragment by him, addressed to Poseidon, and telling of

Poseidon's servants, the dolphins, who had wafted the poet safely to land, when he had lost his course at sea. A fable grew up that certain wicked sailors had thrown Arion overboard, and that the dolphins, charmed by his songs, had saved him. **Ibycus,** of Rhegium in South Italy (540), was closely akin as a poet to Stesichorus. His choral hymns were on like subjects, about heroic wars, and had the same epic character of style. He also wrote love-poems. The story went that Ibycus was murdered at sea, but that his murderers were found out through some cranes that followed the ship; and these 'cranes of Ibycus' became a proverb for the agency of the gods in revealing crime.

24. In the Persian Wars the Greeks had for the first time to fight as one people against a foreign foe. The Greeks beat back the Persians. After this great victory, Greece was safer, and the Greek cities everywhere became more prosperous. One result of the Persian Wars was to make the Greeks in Sicily and Asia and all over the world feel that they were **one people** with the same interests. Another result was to make **Athens** the most popular and powerful city in Greece. The people of Attica were the most gifted of the Ionian race; and the political importance of Athens now gave a large opening to the Athenian genius.

25. **Simonides**, of the Ionian island of Ceos, was born in 556 B.C. and died in 468 B.C. He spent some time at Athens in the reign of Hipparchus; then he visited Thessaly. About 478 he came to Athens again, and finally he went to the court of Hieron, tyrant of Syracuse. His great fame is connected with the time of the Persian Wars, 480—478 B.C. He writes his lyrics in the Dorian dialect, and belongs, as regards lyric form, to the choral Dorian school. But he was by birth an Ionian, and wrote elegiacs in the Ionic dialect. And his highest renown is associated with that of Athens. Thus in him Ionian genius and Dorian art meet at Athens, and he marks a new era—**the beginning of a lyric poetry addressed to all Greece**, taking its spring from Athens, the future centre of Greek intellectual life. His fragments represent hymns to the gods, paeans, odes on victors in the

games, dirges, and other lyric varieties. His elegiac epitaphs on those who fell at the battles of Thermopylae and Salamis are admirable. But nothing that remains of his poetry is more beautiful than a fragment of a dirge, describing Danae with her infant son Perseus, when her father Acrisius has sent her adrift in an ark on the sea; and as darkness comes and the storm arises, the lonely mother gazes on the fair sleeping child.

26. **Bacchylides**, the nephew of Simonides, lived, like his uncle, at Hieron's court, and used the choral lyric style with brilliant grace and finish, but in a lower strain. His fragments, which are of various kinds, often show a certain enthusiasm for the bright pleasures of peaceful life, and we might even fancy that we saw in him a reaction from the warlike spirit called forth by the struggle with Persia.

27. **Pindar** was born, about 522 B.C., at the village of Cynoscephalae near Thebes in Boeotia. He was of a noble family, the Aegidae, who had borne a part in the oldest wars of Sparta. Thus, though he grew up in an Aeolian land, he was connected in blood with the Dorians. The art of flute-playing was hereditary in his house; for, in these great days of Greece, a noble art, such as music, was cherished by the noblest as the gift of the gods. The story went that in his youth he was defeated in a poetical competition by the Theban poetess Corinna. Subsequently he showed her a poem in which, acting on her own hint, he had used Theban mythology. But he had been too profuse. 'You ought to sow with the hand, not with the sack,' said Corinna. Pindar had lessons too from the musician Lāsus of Hermione. He began his poetical career at the age of twenty, with an ode on a Thessalian youth's victory in the games. He grew to be the national lyrist of Greece. It is a sign of the coming time that he also pays his homage to Athens,—'the bulwark of Hellas,' the city that 'laid the foundation of freedom.' He was honoured by the Dorian princes of Sicily—Hieron of Syracuse and Theron of Acragas—and visited them, but declined to make Sicily his permanent home. He was held in veneration

throughout Greece; and received the distinction of being regularly invited to the sacred banquet (*theoxenia*) given at Delphi to the embassies who attended the festivals of Apollo. He died at the age of 79, in 443 B.C. An iron chair in which he had sat was preserved in the temple at Delphi. Two conquerors of Thebes,—the Spartan king Pausanias in the Peloponnesian War, and Alexander the Great—

'bade spare
The house of Pindarus, when temple and tower
Went to the ground.'

28. The remains of Pindar's work represent almost every kind of lyric poem. The fragments may be classified as follows: 1. *Hymns* to Persephone, to Fortune, and in praise of Thebes and its gods. 2. *Paeans* to Apollo of Delphi and Zeus of Dodona. 3. *Choral dithyrambs* to Dionysus. 4. *Processional songs*, for the people of Delos and of Aegina. 5. *Choral songs for maidens*—one addressed to 'Pan, lord of Arcadia, watcher of the awful shrine' (of Cybele). 6. *Choral dance-songs*—'hyporchemes,' as the Greeks called them, in which the words were accompanied by a lively dance or pantomime expressive of the action; they arose from the early Cretan war-dances, and were used especially in the worship of Apollo, as a relief to the solemn paean. One of these was written for the Thebans, and was connected with a propitiatory rite following an eclipse of the sun, probably in 463 B.C. 7. *Encomia*—laudatory odes (in praise of men, and thus distinguished from *hymns* in praise of gods) sung by the festive troop or *comus*. 8. *Scolia*—festive songs to be sung at banquets by a *comus* or festive troop. 9. *Dirges*, to be sung to the flute, with choral dance.

29. Besides the fragments, we have forty-four complete *Epinicia*, or **Odes of Victory**, in which Pindar celebrated victories in great national games. Fourteen odes belong to the games at **Olympia**, held once in four years. The prize was a wreath of wild olive. Twelve odes belong to the **Pythian** games, held at Delphi in honour of Apollo, once in four years, in the 3rd year of each

Olympiad: the prize was a wreath of laurel. Seven odes belong to the Nemean games, held at **Nemea** in honour of Zeus, once in two years, the 2nd and 4th of each Olympiad: the prize was a wreath of pine. Eleven odes belong to the **Isthmian** games, held at the Isthmus of Corinth, in honour of Poseidon, once in two years, in the 1st and 3rd years of each Olympiad: the prize was a wreath of parsley. Among all these odes of which the dates can be fixed, the earliest is the 10th Pythian, in 502 B.C.; the latest, the 5th Olympian, in 452 B.C. The dialect is *epic* with a strong Dorian colouring, and a few Aeolic forms. The music was of a different character in different odes. Where it was *Dorian*, the poetry is most serene and elevated, and the mythical stories are most fully treated: where it was *Aeolian*, the odes are rapid, free, careless, gay: where it was *Lydian*, the poem has a gentle or suppliant tone, as in approaching a temple or altar.

30. The ode of victory was sometimes recited at the place where the games were held, on the evening of the contest; as when at Olympia 'the lovely light of the fair-faced moon beamed forth, and all the holy place sounded with festal joy': sometimes on the victor's return to his native city, either at a banquet, or during a procession to a temple. The odes differ much in style and length. Thus the last Olympian ode, on a boy's victory in the boys' short foot-race, consists of only 19 lines, being merely a thanksgiving to the Graces, in whose temple it is sung. The fourth Pythian ode, in honour of a victory gained in the chariot-race by Arcesilas, king of the Greek colony of Cyrene in Africa, is of 299 lines, and includes a grand epic story in lyric form,—the story of Jason sailing in the ship Argo to Colchis, and, with Medea's help, bringing back the golden fleece. This ode was brought out at Cyrene with a splendid chorus.

31. **Pindar's Treatment of the Myths.** Pindar seldom dwells much on the details of any particular victory. In the case of the chariot-race, the most important contest of all, it was not easy to connect the actual victory with the personal merit of the owner, unless he had also been the driver. Pindar usually takes

some heroic legend or group of legends connected with the victor or the victor's city, and makes this his main theme. Thus, in the fourth Pythian, the link between Jason's story and the king of Cyrene is found in the tradition that Cyrene had been colonised from the island of Thera by the descendants of one of Jason's comrades. In treating the legends, Pindar aims especially at bringing out their *moral*, and applying this to the victor or his city. If we wish to understand Pindar's place among his contemporaries, we must never forget how closely these legends which he interpreted were bound up with Greek religion, and with the belief of Greek cities and great Greek families about their own origin.

32. The loss of the music by which Pindar's Odes were accompanied deprives us of an indispensable aid to the comprehension of their effect as works of art. And, if the music were extant, modern imagination would still have to supply the scenic accessories of a gorgeous festival, the light, the colour, the movement, the glowing sympathy of a brilliant audience with the newly won or freshly remembered victory which shed a reflected lustre on the victor's native city, the thrill of patriotic pride responding to each allusion, faint or dark, perhaps, for us, that touched some household word of inherited renown, the sense of deepened spiritual life with which Greeks for whom the faith of their fathers was still a vital force heard the secret lessons of divine lore drawn forth by that great poet of all Greece in whom the priests of the Delphian Apollo revered the full inspiration of their god. Pindar's achievement cannot be measured by a literary criticism of his text. The glory of his song has passed for ever from the world with the sound of the rolling harmonies on which it once was borne, with the splendour of rushing chariots and athletic forms around which it threw its radiance, with the white-pillared cities by the Aegean or Sicilian sea in which it wrought its spell, with the beliefs or joys which it ennobled; but those who love his poetry, and who strive to enter into its high places, can still know that they breathe a pure and bracing air, and can still feel vibrating through a clear calm

sky the strong pulse of the eagle's wings as he soars with steady eyes against the sun.

33. Thus the two greatest lyric poets, Simonides and Pindar, carried Lyric Poetry into a wider field. With them, while it is mainly Dorian in form, it ceases to belong, by spirit, to any one division of the Greek people. It begins to speak to all the Greeks about those great traditions and deeds which make up the common faith and fame. And now the law of natural growth which goes all through Greek literature calls on another branch of the Greek race to do its part.

Note

1. For this stanza the writer is indebted to the kindness of Mr. Tennyson.

PART II—THE ATTIC LITERATURE

4

THE DRAMA

Tragedy. Aeschylus, 525—456 B.C. Sophocles, 495—405 B.C. Euripides, 480—406 B.C.

The Old Comedy. Aristophanes, 448—385 B.C. *The Middle Comedy,* 390—320 B.C.; The *New Comedy,* 320—250 B.C.

1. The people of Attica belonged to the Ionian race, but had a stamp of their own which distinguished them from the Ionians in the colonies of Asia Minor. Aristotle remarked that the Greek temperament, like the Greek climate, is a happy mean between its neighbours on west and east; the Greek is more intelligent than the brave European, and more manly than the subtle Asiatic. The like might be said of the Attic temperament as compared with those two others which form the great standing contrast in Greek history, the Ionian and the Dorian. The Athenian mind has the elasticity and bright grace of the Ionian. It has the fortitude and sober intelligence of the Dorian. But it is not, like the Ionian, effeminate, nor, like the Dorian, rigid. The Attic language is like the Attic mind, flexible without too much softness, precise and vigorous without harshness. The Epic poetry of the Ionians and the choral Lyric poetry of the Dorians were blended by the Attic genius in a new poetical form, which has more varied interest, but which also demands more various power, than any other—the *drama.* Artistic drama was the creation of Athens.

2. **Origin of Drama.** From early times, we saw, the Greek conceived his deities as men and women, with more than human power, but susceptible of human joy or sorrow, malice or partisanship. The more a Greek entered into the spirit of his religion, the more personal sympathy he would feel with his gods' joy or sorrow. Now, among all the Greek gods, there was none that appealed to human sympathy more vividly than **Dionysus**, the god of wine, the giver of physical joy and excitement, the enemy of everything that can darken or deaden the vital spirit in man. Dionysus was described as traversing the earth in a progress full of danger and anguish and triumph, as overcoming bitter foes divine or human, as establishing his worship in India, in Asia, in Greece; and through these legends there ran a mystic undercurrent of allusion to a place where those who have been faithful on earth shall drink after death of a cup stronger and sweeter than wine.

3. His **festivals** belonged to the season when the grapes were gathered,—when the wine-press was busy,—when, in mid-winter, last year's cask was tapped,—or when the return of spring brought the first sunshine for the vines. In December the people of Attica kept the Vintage Feast,—the 'Lesser' or 'Rural' Dionysia; in January, the Feast of the Wine-press (*Lenaea*); in February, the *Anthesteria*, the merry 'Feast of Flowers,' when last year's wine was opened; and in March, the Great Dionysia. The last three were kept at Athens, the first was kept in the country. Imagine, then, the people of an Attic village gathered together to keep the Vintage Feast of Dionysus at the foot of the warm, vine-clad hills. There is a rustic altar of wood or turf. Rustic singers gather round it to sing a hymn in honour of the god, relating some of his well-known adventures. The story said that Dionysus was attended in his wanderings by certain woodland beings, the *satyrs*, with long pointed ears, snub noses, and goats' tails. It would be natural for the rustic worshippers, singing of the god's fortunes, to feign that they themselves were such satyrs, to speak of his victory or suffering as if they had seen it. This would seem to bring them nearer to their god.

4. And then, in their yearning to imagine his deeds more vividly, another step would soon be taken. The leader of the chorus would enact the character of Dionysus himself, or of a messenger from him. He would relate some exploit of the god, or some danger which the god had gone through. The chorus would then express in song the feelings which the recital awakened. Here, then, we should have the **first germ of drama**—that is of **poetry, not in narrative only, like epic, but in action**. The choral hymn sung to Dionysus on such occasions was called the **dithyramb**. From the dithyramb sprang both *Tragedy* and *Comedy*. **Tragedy** means the 'goat-song,' because a goat was sacrificed to Dionysus before the choral hymn was sung. **Comedy** means the 'village-song,' this same hymn looked at from another point of view, as bringing out the jests of a rustic carnival. But this chorus must at first have been of a very rude kind,—little more than a rustic band of revellers led by a flute-player. The musician and poet ARION (600 B.C.) was the first to give the dithyramb a regular lyric form. He arranged it to be sung at the festivals of Dionysus by a trained chorus of fifty persons, grouped round the altar, and hence called a *cyclic* or circular chorus.

5. This artistic chorus to Dionysus first came in among the Dorians. But it was in Attica that the next steps were taken. **Thespis** (536 B.C.) was a leader of dithyrambic choruses, who made a slight improvement by arranging that the dialogue about Dionysus should be no longer between the leader and the whole chorus, but between the leader and one member of the chorus specially appointed for that purpose. The leader or **coryphaeus** stood on a raised platform, and in the pauses of the choral song held a dialogue with this one member of the chorus, who was called the *answerer,* (*hypocrĭtes*),—afterwards the ordinary Greek word for **actor**. Thespis must not be regarded as the founder of Tragedy. The story that he went about the country with a company of strolling players, acting his plays on a *waggon,* comes from a confusion. In the processions of

Dionysus and Demeter, there was free licence of rough jesting among the crowd; and *jokes from a cart* became proverbial.

6. **Phrynichus** of Athens (512—476) still used only one actor, but improved the organisation of the chorus, sometimes subdividing it into smaller bands, one of which might represent a group of maidens, another a group of elders, or the like. One of his choral performances represented the *Capture of Miletus*, the chief town of Ionia, in the last year of the Ionian Revolt (494 B.C.). The Athenians were so moved, Herodotus says, that they fined the poet, who had set before them the sufferings of their kinsmen, 'for reminding them of their own misfortunes.' In his *Phoenissae* (476 B.C.) Phrynichus celebrated the deeds of Athens in the Persian Wars: one group of the chorus represented Phoenician women who had been sent to the Persian court, while another group represented Persian elders.

7. **'Satyric' Pieces**. The satyrs, or goat-like attendants of Dionysus, still kept their old place in his traditional worship. And as the choral performance became more refined and artistic, a special entertainment was set apart for the purpose of bringing in these grotesque beings. In this the chorus represented satyrs, as in the early days of the dithyramb. CHOERILUS (524—465 B.C.) of Athens is named as 'king of the Satyr-play'; and it was further developed by PRATÎNAS (500—460 B.C.) a Dorian of Phlius who came to Athens.

8. **Aeschylus**, the real **founder of Tragedy**, was an Athenian of the township of Eleusis, and was born in 525 B.C. The family of his father Euphorion was ancient and distinguished. At the age of 25, in 500 B.C., Aeschylus competed for the tragic prize with Pratinas; but Phrynichus was his chief rival in his earlier career. Either then or soon afterwards he brought in the change which first created true drama. The 'tragedy' which Aeschylus found existing was a sacred choral entertainment somewhat like a modern oratorio, in which the choral song and music were occasionally relieved by the recitative of a single actor, or by dialogue between this actor and the leader of the Chorus.

Aeschylus introduced **a second actor**. The dialogue now became independent of the Chorus. The two actors, by varying their parts, could act a complete story from beginning to end. The Chorus took part in this action by giving counsel or encouragement to the actors, or by uttering the feelings which the events would move in a thoughtful spectator. Hitherto the dialogue had been secondary to the choral song. Now **the choral song became secondary to the dialogue. Drama is now mature**: since now a complete action can be represented as passing before the eye. We have seven great tragedies by Aeschylus. But before we can understand these, we must have some notion of what a performance in a Greek theatre was like.

9. **Tragedy** was acted at three of the four Dionysiac festivals, the Lesser Dionysia, the Lenaea, and the Greater Dionysia. But the production of a *new* tragedy always took place either at the Lenaea or at the Greater Dionysia. A poet's first object was to get a chorus. Several tragic choruses were required for each festival. Citizens, chosen from the ten Attic tribes in turn, paid for the dresses and for the musical training of the choruses. This was a costly but a very popular public service. Men vied with each other in doing it handsomely: a tragic chorus sometimes cost about £120, equivalent to many times that sum now: and the *chorêgus* whose chorus was best trained and dressed got a prize. The 'Street of Tripods' at Athens was adorned with monuments of such victories, and we still have the beautiful monument of Lysicrates, chorêgus in 335 B.C. A poet who wished to bring out a tragedy applied to the ' King Archon,' who had the control of the sacred festivals, for a chorus. If this was granted, the poet had next to train it, and to get his actors. In the early days of tragic art, the tragic poet often acted himself. Later, professional actors were paid by the State, and the poets sometimes cast lots for a chief actor, who then chose his own subordinates. A *third* actor was first used by Sophocles in 468 B.C., and one of his late plays, the *Oedipus at Colonus*, requires a fourth actor. 'Mute persons,' such as guards,

servants, & c., could be brought on the stage in addition to the regular actors. The women's parts were acted by men. When the principal character in the piece is a woman, the chorus is composed of women; unless the poet wishes, for artistic reasons, to *isolate* the heroine, as in the *Antigone* of Sophocles, where the chorus consists of Theban Elders.

10. A **trilogy** was a group of three tragedies. A **tetralogy** was a group of three tragedies with a satyr-drama added to them. We are told that Aeschylus was the first who set the example of competing for the prize with three tragedies,—acted successively, and representing subjects connected with each other,—followed by a satyr-drama. Three plays of Aeschylus,—the Agamemnon, the Choephori, and the Eumenides,—form the only extant example of such a trilogy. They are usually called collectively the *Oresteia,* i.e. 'the story of Orestes': but the Athenians seem to have given this name only to the Choephori, or to the Choephori with the Eumenides. Sophocles 'began the custom of contending with a single play, and not a tetralogy': and this is explained to mean that, though he brought out tetralogies, the four pieces composing each of them were not connected in subject. It is probable that the tragic poet did not always or necessarily bring out a trilogy, but might also compete with a single tragedy: under what conditions, however, we cannot tell.

11. **The Greek Theatre.** The early tragic choruses had performed on a temporary wooden platform, sometimes in the market-place. There was an old proverb for a bad place at a spectacle,—'A view from the poplar,'—because people used to climb a poplar tree near the market-place when they could not get seats. Once this platform gave way,—in 500 B.C., it is said, when Aeschylus and Pratînas were competing—and it was then decided to build a more lasting stage in honour of the god Dionysus. The famous Theatre of Dionysus was begun about 500 B.C. It was in the form of a half-circle, open to the sky, and was situated on a piece of ground, sacred to Dionysus, called the *Lenaeon,* or *Place of the Wine-press,* at the foot of the

Acropolis on its south-east side. The upper tiers of seats for the spectators were hewn out of the natural rock of the Acropolis; the lower tiers were made artificially of wood or stone; and a stage was built of stone, with a high back wall to shut it in.

12. Now imagine yourself sitting in one of the upper tiers of seats, with your back to the Acropolis and your face towards Mount Hymettus where it slopes to the sea, looking down into the theatre. The house can easily hold upwards of 20,000 people, and we hear of as many as 30,000 being present. That long, very narrow platform is what we should call the *stage,* and what the Greeks called the *speaking-place,* because the dialogue of the actors was held upon it. The high wall at the back of the stage is the *scene.* In Tragedy, the hangings or painted wood-work with which it is covered represent usually a temple or a palace; in Comedy, a street of Athens or a private house. There are three doors in it, through which the actors pass in and out. The long stage, you see, is much too narrow for such crowded spectacles or complicated effects as are seen on the deep modern stages.

13. At the middle point of the stage, some steps—known as 'Charon's staircase,' because the ghost sometimes comes up by them—lead down into what we should call the *pit.* The Greeks call it the *orchestra* or dancing-place. It is a semicircle, bounded by the lowest row of seats and by the stage. No spectators are admitted to it. It is kept exclusively for the chorus. The altar which you see in the middle of the orchestra is the *thymele* or altar of Dionysus. It will form the central point of the choral dances.

14. The lowest tier of seats, immediately round the orchestra, contains 67 stalls of white marble, reserved for priests and magistrates, and is divided into 13 compartments by passages which run the whole way up to the topmost row of seats, so as to cut the theatre into 13 wedge-like segments. There is also a broad cross-passage, dividing the upper block of tiers from the lower. The place of honour, exactly in the centre of the lowest

half-circle, is occupied by the priest of Dionysus, with the priest of Apollo on his right, and on his left the priest of Zeus Polieus, or 'Guardian of the City.' The theatre is a sacred place; both Tragedy and Comedy are acts of public worship.

15. The **general effect of a Greek tragedy** was unlike anything on the modern stage. It depended chiefly on two things. First, the story represented was one which the whole audience knew in its main outlines, and which they regarded as *sacred*, since the persons were the gods and heroes of their race. Secondly, there was little animated gesture or movement on the stage. The two or three actors stood there more like a group of majestic statues. They wore masks; for the calm grandeur of Greek tragedy could dispense with animated play of feature, which would, indeed, have been lost on the spectators in so large a space. In a play like *Oedipus the King*, where Oedipus puts out his own eyes, this would not happen on the stage, but would be related by a messenger, and Oedipus would come on in a different mask. The tragic actor was made up to look larger than human with the long tragic mask, a sort of high wig, padding, and very thick-soled boots or *buskins*. Hence Milton speaks of tragedy as 'the buskin'd stage'—but alludes to Ben Jonson's comedies as 'Jonson's learned *sock*,' because the ancient comic actors wore slippers (*socci*).

16. The **costume** of tragic actors was usually of one general character,—that which was worn at processions or festivals of the god Dionysus: a striped robe falling in folds to the feet, often with a long train, with a high, broad band or girdle; over this, a mantle ('chlamys,' the Roman *palla*) of bright colour. This general type of costume could be varied so as to express the different conditions of the persons, but the sacred, festal character was always kept; it was never, in the classical days, *merely* theatrical. Partial changes of side-scenery could be effected by 'the revolving doors,' as they were called, triangular prisms on pivots at the sides of the stage. Changes of the whole back-scene occur nowhere in tragedy, except in the *Ajax* of

Sophocles, and in the *Eumenides* (perhaps, too, *Choephori*) of Aeschylus; when a curtain would be drawn up (not dropped) to conceal the operation. There were mechanical contrivances for suspending gods in the air, and for showing the interior of a house through the open central door.

17. **Structure of a Tragedy.** The first part of the dialogue, before the chorus came in, was called the *prologue*. The song of the chorus, as they marched into the orchestra and took their place, was called the *parodos*. Each choral song which they afterwards sang at their station was called a *stasimon*. An *episode* was the portion of the play contained between any two *stasima*. The part after the last *stasimon* to the end was the *exodus*. A lyric dirge, in which the actor on the stage and the chorus in the orchestra both took part, was called a *commus*. The songs of the chorus practically divide the tragedy into acts, usually about four or five in number. The shortest Greek tragedy that we have contains less than 900 lines; the longest, upwards of 1700.

18. Suppose that we are in the Theatre of Dionysus at the great festival of the god: there is an audience of some 25,000, not only Athenian citizens and women (the latter placed apart from the men in the upper rows), but Greeks from other cities, and ambassadors seated near the priests and magistrates in the places next the orchestra. We are to see the *Eumenides* or *Furies* of Aeschylus. The orchestra is empty at present. The *scene*, or wall behind the stage, represents the temple of Apollo at Delphi. It has three doors. Enter, from the middle or 'royal' door, the aged priestess of Apollo; she wears a long striped robe, and over her shoulders a saffron mantle. Pilgrims are waiting to consult the oracle; and she speaks a prayer before she goes into the inner chamber of the temple, to take her place on the three-footed throne, round which vapours rise from the cavern beneath. Then she passes into the shrine through the central door.

19. But she quickly returns in horror. A murderer, she says, is kneeling there, and the ghastly Furies, his pursuers, are asleep

around him. As she quits the stage by the side-door on the right, two figures come forth by the central door, as if from the inner shrine. One of them wears the costume of the Pythian festival at Delphi,—a long tunic, gaily striped, with sleeves, and a light mantle of purple, hanging from the shoulders. In his left hand he has a golden bow. This is the god Apollo himself. The other figure is clad with much less splendour; at his back hangs loosely the petasus, a broad-brimmed hat worn by hunters or shepherds or wayfarers; in one hand he bears a long branch of laurel, the symbol of the suppliant, in the other, a drawn sword. This is Orestes, who has slain his mother Clytaemnestra, the murderess of his father Agamemnon, and has sought refuge with Apollo from the pursuing Furies. A silent figure moves behind these two; it is the god Hermes, carrying in his hand the herald's staff, decked with white ribbons. Apollo bids Hermes escort Orestes to Athens, to seek the judgment of the goddess Athene.

20. The ghost of Clytaemnestra now moves into the orchestra, and mounts the stage. She calls on the sleeping Furies within, and then vanishes. They wake to find Orestes gone, and dash on the stage in wild rage—haggard forms with sable robes, snaky locks, and blood-shot eyes. Apollo appears, and drives them from his shrine. Now the scene changes to Athens. Meanwhile the Furies have taken their station as chorus in the orchestra, and, in grand choral songs, declare their mission as Avengers of blood. Athene assembles a Court of Athenians on the Hill of Ares, (the real Hill of Ares was not half a mile off, on the S.W. side of the Acropolis), and thus founds the famous Court of the Areopagus. The Furies arraign Orestes; Apollo defends him. The votes of the judges are equally divided. Athene's casting vote acquits Orestes. The wrath of the Furies now threatens Athens. But Athene at last prevails on them to accept a shrine in her land,—a cave beneath the Hill of Ares; and the play ends with this great reconciliation, as a procession of torch-bearers escort the Furies to their new home.

21. Thus a Greek tragedy could bring before a vast Greek audience, in a grandly simple form, harmonized by choral music and dance, the great figures of their religious and civil history: the god Apollo in his temple at Delphi, the goddess Athene in the act of founding the Court of the Areopagus, the Furies passing to their shrine beneath the hill, the hero Orestes on his trial. The picture had at once ideal beauty of the highest kind and, for Greeks, a deep reality; they seemed to be looking at the actual *beginning* of those rites and usages which were most dear and sacred in their daily life.

22. **The Tragedies of Aeschylus.** The great artists of old Greece, who gave themselves wholly to their art, were prolific: 70 tragedies, besides satyric dramas, are ascribed to Aeschylus in the 40 years of his poetical life; 113 to Sophocles; 92 to Euripides; and to one tragic poet, who has left only fragments, no less than 240. From Aeschylus we have only seven tragedies left. The *Persae,* brought out in 472 B.C., is a magnificent dramatic song of triumph for the victory of Greece over the invading host of Persia. Aeschylus had himself fought at Marathon, at Salamis, at Artemisium and at Plataea. The spirit of a soldier glows in the splendid description of the battle of Salamis, with that trumpet-call ringing above it, *Go forth, sons of the Greeks, free your country, free your children and wives, and the shrines of your ancestral gods, and the tombs of your fathers.* Nor is a deep moral wanting; the spirit of Darius rises from the grave to tell the nobles of Persia that, in this ruin, the gods are punishing the insolence of Xerxes.

23. In the *Seven against Thebes* (468 B.C.) we are shown how the inherited curse in the house of Oedipus is visited on his sons Eteocles and Polyneices, who slay each other in single combat when the Argives, under Adrastus, besiege Thebes. Warriors splendid in their panoply gleam, as it were, under a sky lurid with the lightnings of angry gods. The *Prometheus Bound* (of uncertain date, perhaps 472—468 B.C.) is a sublime picture of the superhuman being who had stolen fire from heaven, and

taught the elements of civilisation to men, chained to a cliff in the Caucasus by command of Zeus, the new king of the gods, Prometheus knows a secret on which the throne of Zeus depends; but, amid his tortures, no threats will make him utter it. As he speaks his last defiance, the thunders of Zeus break forth, and the scene closes with the crash of an appalling tempest.

24. The *Suppliants* (462 B.C.) are the fifty daughters of Danaus, who have fled with their father from Egypt to Argos, in order to avoid marrying their first-cousins, the fifty sons of Aegyptus. The Argive king Pelasgus receives and protects them. The *Agamemnon, Choephori,* and *Eumenides,* were the crown of the poet's work. They were brought out at Athens in 458 B.C., two years before his death. In the *Agamemnon,* we have the return of the victorious king from Troy to Mycenae, and his murder by Clytaemnestra. The *Choephori,* or 'offerers of libations,' are Electra, daughter of Agamemnon, and her handmaids, bringing offerings to her father's grave. Her prayer is heard. Orestes returns to Mycenae, and slays Clytaemnestra and her paramour Aegisthus. In the *Eumenides,* as we have seen, Orestes is accused by the Furies, defended by Apollo, and absolved by Athene.

25. **Religious and Moral Ideas of Aeschylus.** Aeschylus felt profoundly the seeming war of principles in the moral government of the world. When the wicked prospered and the guiltless suffered others might be content to say, 'The god is a blind, malignant force.' Aeschylus strove to go farther back. Somewhere, if we could only reach it, he felt, there is a higher unity in which the seeming strife is resolved. True, those bright gods of Olympus above, who send us joy and health, who are so full of loving-kindness and wise providence, seem to rule on different principles from the dark, terrible gods of the nether world, who send plague or famine to blight us, whose joy is in drinking blood, who are the ministers of pain and death. Yet let us look deeper, and we shall see that both the gods of heaven

and the gods infernal are working out one law. *That law is the law of righteousness.* A power above the gods themselves, even *Necessity,* ordains that no offence against Righteousness shall remain unpunished.

26. A man is very rich and great; he grows arrogant. The gods begin to be *jealous* of him. He sins. The gods blind his heart. He goes on from crime to crime. At last his measure is full. Fate forges a sword and puts it into the hand of the Fury; Justice gives the word; and the sinner is smitten. Sometimes the enormous sin of the father is even visited on his children. A curse descends from generation to generation. An Avenging Fury becomes the silent inmate of the house. After long years, perhaps, some act of insolence done by the inheritor of the curse puts him in the Fury's grasp, and she claims from him the whole debt. Thus the gods slowly teach men that sin entails suffering. Even in sleep a remembrance of anguish is busy at the heart, painfully instilling the lesson of virtue. Nay, the younger gods themselves have been thus disciplined by Necessity. Zeus, when he had overthrown an elder dynasty, at first abused his power. But Necessity taught him that he stood in need of wisdom, and must master, not by violence, the secret of Prometheus.

Thus in Aeschylus we are led up to the mysterious sources of divine and moral law. The war between the gods of heaven and hell is found to be no longer implacable, since both, constrained by Necessity and aided by her daemonic ministers, are working in the cause of Righteousness.

27. Aeschylus was the tragic poet of all Greece rather than that of Athens alone. He had fought in those great wars against Persia which had first made the Greeks everywhere feel that they were one people; and in his poetry he spoke to all the Greeks alike. He said that his plays were only morsels from Homer's banquet; and he is indeed the dramatist of that heroic age in which the traditions of all the Greeks meet. His heroes, as in the *Iliad,* stand above common humanity. He has the true

Homeric feeling for the majesty of kings, whose sceptres are given to them by Zeus, and who are royal even among the dead. After the Persian wars, as Athens grew more democratic, it probably became less congenial to Aeschylus. He may have felt, too, after the victory of his younger rival Sophocles in 468 B.C., that his poetry was ceasing to be in sympathy with the rising generation. Much of his later life was spent away from Athens, chiefly with Hieron of Syracuse, whose foundation of Catana, about 476 B.C., he celebrated in a lost play *The Women of Aetna.* In his *Eumenides* we see his political feeling towards the close of his life. He does honour to Theseus, the hero of the *old* Athenian democracy. But he warns the *new* democracy against enfeebling the conservative Areopagus, the 'safeguard of the city,' or taking away its old right of watching over public morals. Aeschylus died at Gela in Sicily, in 456 B.C., aged 69.

28. **Sophocles**, son of Sophilus, was born probably in 495 B.C. His family belonged to the township of Colonus, near Athens; that Colonus where, in one of his great tragedies, he makes the weary Oedipus find rest,—where the nightingale haunts the green glades, constant to the dark-veined ivy,—where narcissus and golden crocus bloom, where the springs of clear water never fail; a region hallowed by the joyous presence of the god Dionysus and loved by the Muses. Sophocles was fifteen years of age when the Greeks overthrew the Persians in the great sea-fight at Salamis, and was chosen to lead the paean sung by a chorus of boys before the trophy raised to commemorate that victory. He had lessons from the famous musician Lamprus; and in 468, at the age of twenty-seven, competed for the prize of tragedy against Aeschylus, his elder by just thirty years. The house was divided, we are told, on the merits of the rivals. The presiding archon left the decision to Cimon, who had just come back from his victories in Thrace, and to the other nine generals. They gave the prize to Sophocles.

29. From that time to his death he was the favourite tragic poet of Athens. The first prize fell to him no less than twenty

times. The average merit of his pieces, and of his competitors, may be judged from the fact that *Oedipus the King* got only a second prize. In 440 B.C., after his great triumph with the Antigone, he was appointed one of the ten Generals who, with Pericles, were to reduce the revolt of Samos,—an instance of the public honour paid at Athens to poetical genius, and, in this case, probably a sign of general faith in the poet's practical gifts. The only cloud on his long, brilliant life seems to have been a transient one. His son Iophon, resenting the partiality of Sophocles for a son and a grandson by a second marriage, is said to have arraigned him before their clansmen as being incapable of managing property. Sophocles, the story adds, was content to disprove his imbecility by reading the chorus from his *Oedipus at Colonus,* in which he praises his native place.

30. Genius, beauty of person, piety, a sweet nature, and a happy fortune made Sophocles seem to the Athenians a man loved by the gods. In his boyhood he had sung the paean that was as a prelude to the great career of Athens; and he died, in 405 B.C., just before that career was closed by the battle of Aegospotami. *He has died well,* a poet wrote of him some months later, *having suffered no evil.* And Aristophanes, in a piece composed at the time, imagines Sophocles in the underworld, standing aside from the noisy rivalries of the dead,—*gentle in the shades, even as he was gentle among us.*

To be worshipped after death as a hero was nearly the equivalent, in old Greece, for being canonized as a saint. This worship the Athenians paid to Sophocles, honouring his memory with yearly sacrifice.

31. In about 60 years, Sophocles wrote upwards of 100 plays, of which only seven remain. The play called the *Trachiniae* or *Women of Trachis,* because these form the chorus, tells how Deianeira, living at Trachis in Thessaly, learns that Heracles has fallen in love with Iolê, and sends him a robe anointed with the blood of the Centaur Nessus, knowing not that it is aught but a harmless love-charm; and how Heracles, in mortal torment

from the poison, bids his son Hyllus take him to the top of Mount Oeta, and lay him on a funeral pyre; and thence, 'wrapped in heavenly flame, is gathered to the host of the gods.' It has been doubted whether the play is by Sophocles, but groundlessly; if inferior to some of his plays, it is still one of the finest and most dramatically constructed of extant tragedies. The *Ajax* opens on the morning after Ajax—in the frenzy with which Athene punished his pride,—has butchered the cattle of the Greeks, thinking that he was slaying the Greek chiefs who had slighted him by giving the armour of Achilles to Odysseus. When reason returns, he is overwhelmed with the sense of dishonour, and kills himself. The *Electra* shows us the vengeance taken by Orestes on his mother Clytaemnestra and on Aegisthus,—the theme treated in the *Choephori* of Aeschylus and the *Electra* of Euripides; but has a clearer artistic unity than the former, and more ideal beauty than the latter.

32. *Oedipus the King* is, in subtlety of structure, the masterpiece among extant Greek plays. Oedipus, the great, the wise, has delivered Thebes from the Sphinx by guessing her riddle, has been raised, though an alien, to the throne, and has married the widow of the late King Laius. A pestilence comes on the city; and when the Thebans ask the oracle at Delphi how they can be healed, the god Apollo bids them investigate and punish the murder of Laius, who was slain on the road to Delphi. Oedipus takes up the search with zeal. Step by step it is proved, first that he himself was the unwitting murderer of Laius; next, that he was the murdered man's son, and that, therefore, his wife is his mother. In the frenzy of his horror he puts out his own eyes. When the *Oedipus at Colonus* opens, some years have passed. Oedipus has been driven from Thebes by Creon, (now king) with the consent of his own sons, Eteocles and Polyneices. Attended by his daughters, Antigone and Ismene, he finds an asylum at Athens with King Theseus; he wins peace and pardon from the gods; and at last, called by the voice of one unseen, he passes from earth in strange wise, beheld of Theseus alone.

33. The *Antigone* is a yet later chapter in the story of the house. The two sons of Oedipus, Polyneices, the assailant of Thebes, and Eteocles, its champion, have slain each other in single combat. Creon, king of Thebes, has decreed that no one, on pain of death, shall pay the rites of burial to Polyneices; but Antigone sets the unwritten law of the gods above the edict of man, and renders the last honours to her brother's corpse, and is put to death by Creon; whose son, the lover of Antigone, and that son's mother, slay themselves, cursing him.

The scene of the *Philoctetes* (409 B.C.) is laid on the desolate isle of Lemnos. Ten years ago, the hero Philoctetes, suffering from a noisome wound in the foot, was left there in his sleep by the Greeks, at the instance of Odysseus, as they sailed against Troy; but now they need him, since he has the bow of Heracles, by which alone—so say the gods—Troy can be taken. Odysseus persuades Neoptolemus, the son of Achilles, to help him in a base scheme for seizing Philoctetes, or stealing his bow; the scheme has succeeded, when the young man's better nature revolts against it. If Philoctetes will not come with them to Troy, Neoptolemus will not steal his bow. At this moment, the divine Heracles himself appears; Philoctetes learns the health and glory that await him at Troy; and gladly obeys his summoners.

34. Aeschylus shows us grand heroic forms fulfilling the doom appointed for them by awful supernatural powers: Sophocles is preeminently the dramatist of human character. He excels in delineating the great primary emotions of our nature. The self-sacrificing devotion of Antigone, the victory of youthful generosity over youthful ambition in Neoptolemus, the bitter sense of lost honour in Ajax, the horror in Oedipus of a sudden and overwhelming reverse, are exquisite studies of the human soul to which the artist has, given a typical beauty—expressing what is essentially true in each, marking by a thousand fine touches how intimately he felt the nature which he was drawing, but never using his subtle analysis for the sake of any momentary effect which would mar the repose, disturb the

symmetry and clearness, of Tragedy as he conceived it—that is, as a work which is a failure unless it has artistic breadth and unity, and can bear to be viewed as we view a temple or a group of sculpture, judging it to be good, not because it has clever details, but because it is beautiful as a whole. Sophocles believes in the goodness of the divine agency that governs the world, not because he fails to see any apparent contradictions between his religion and the moral facts of life, nor because he can partly reconcile such conflicts, as Aeschylus did, by belief in a Necessity which controls even the caprices of the gods, but rather because he finds a solution in the analysis of our own nature. The deepest instincts of human nature itself, its affections, its pity, its terror, bear witness to the unity and supremacy of an unwritten but eternal law of purity which is always identical with the true will of the gods, though not always in harmony with man's positive interpretation of that will.

35. Historically, the plays of Sophocles have this special interest, that they interpret, more spiritually than anything else that we have, the higher moral and mental side of the age of Pericles; they have its noble tone of conciliation between sacred tradition and a progressive culture, between authority and reason, between the letter and the spirit of religion. If Sophocles has been, on the whole, less popular in the modern world than either Aeschylus or Euripides, one reason may be this—there is no other Greek poet whose genius belongs so peculiarly to the best Greek time. Aeschylus has an element of Hebrew grandeur, Euripides has strong elements of modern pathos and romance; these things easily come home to us. But in order fully to appreciate Sophocles, we must place ourselves in sympathy with the Greek mind in its most characteristic modes of thought and with the Greek sense of beauty in it highest purity.

36. **Euripides** was born in 480 B.C., the year in which the Greeks conquered the Persians at Salamis. He was therefore forty-five years younger than Aeschylus, and only fifteen years younger than Sophocles. But Euripides is much further from

both Aeschylus and Sophocles than Sophocles is from Aeschylus. He represents a new order of ideas and a different conception of the dramatist's art. His father Mnesarchus, who gave him a liberal education—not a very cheap luxury at Athens—was probably of better birth and fortune than is implied in the jests of Comedy about the poet's mother Clito having been a herb-seller. The young Euripides was meant at first to be a professional athlete; at seventeen he tried painting; at twenty-five he brought out his first tragedy. He was thirty-nine before he gained the first prize; and during a poetical career of nearly fifty years he gained it only five times in all.

37. The comic poet Aristophanes lashed him with unsparing mockery as an atheist, a quibbler, and a bad artist. His domestic life seems to have been unhappy, and his poetry contains many bitter sayings about women, though few could express female emotion more tenderly. The extreme democracy which set in during the Peloponnesian War was not to his taste, and he speaks of the small farmers, who keep clear of the public assembly, as those 'who alone save the country.' Altogether it is not strange that he should have left Athens about 409 B.C., and taken up his abode in Macedonia with Archelaus,—a king whom he compliments on putting down brigands, and who liked to draw clever Greeks to his court. Here Euripides died in 406,—a few months before Sophocles, who honoured his brother poet's memory, in his next tragedy, by forbidding the actors to wear crowns or splendid dresses.

38. Of the 92 dramas that went under the name of Euripides, 75 (including 8 satyr-plays) were thought genuine by the old critics: we have 17.[1] The *Alcestis*, the oldest of these (438 B.C.), tells how Alcestis died to save the life of her husband Admêtus, and was brought back from the grave by Heracles. *Medea* (431 B.C.) is the princess of Colchis, who for love of Jason has shown him how to win the golden fleece, and has fled with him to his own land; but he has forsaken her for Glaucê, daughter of Creon king of Corinth. Medea, by her magic arts, destroys his

bride, slays the children whom she had borne to Jason, and is carried through the air, in an enchanted car, to Athens. The *Hippolytus* (428 B.C.)—a play which gained the first prize—tells how that son of Theseus was cursed by his father, and perished, when his stepmother Phaedra had falsely accused him of assailing her honour; and how Theseus, when his son is dying before his eyes, learns the truth, too late, from Artemis, the goddess of chastity. The play alludes to the recent death of Pericles (429 B.C.). Racine used this plot in his *Phêdre.* The *Hecuba* (425 B.C.) sets forth the vengeance of the widowed queen of Troy on Polymestor, who had slain her son Polydorus and carried off her daughter Polyxena. The *Andromache* (424—422 B.C.?) turns on the fortunes of her who was once Hector's wife and is now the captive of Neoptolemus, son of Achilles. It bears the mark of the Peloponnesian War in a celebrated invective against the Spartan character.

39. The *Ion* (424—421 B.C.), one of the finest plays, of which the scene is laid at Delphi, unfolds how Ion, founder of the Ionian race and of the Attic tribes, was in truth the son of Apollo by Creusa daughter of Erectheus. The glow of feeling for Athenian glory makes this play akin to the three next. We might almost compare the group to those histories which Shakespeare dedicated to the glory of England before he turned to the works of his ripest art. In the *Suppliants* (420—417 B.C.?) Athens appears as the champion of humanity against Creon, king of Thebes, who has refused burial to the Argive warriors slain before its walls. So, too, in the *Heracleidae* (of like date), Athens becomes a city of refuge to the children of Heracles, persecuted by Eurystheus, once their dead father's taskmaster. The *Mad Heracles* (420— 417 B.C.?) tells how Heracles, driven mad by his enemy, the goddess Hera (Juno), murders his wife Megara and his children, and on recovering his senses, is going to kill himself; when king Theseus soothes his despair, and persuades him to seek grace and peace at Athens.

40. *Iphigenia among the Tauri,* a very noble tragedy, of

uncertain date, belongs at least to the poet's later period. The scene is laid at Balaclava in the Crimea. Iphigenia, rescued by the miraculous intervention of Artemis from the death to which her father had doomed her, has become a priestess in the temple of that goddess, where human victims are sacrificed. She is called upon to immolate two strangers, when she discovers them to be her brother Orestes and his friend Pylades. She plans their escape; and finally, by command of the goddess Athene, Thoas, the king of the land, allows all three to go back to Greece, where they found the worship of Artemis at Halae and Brauron in Attica. The *Troads* (415 B.C.) is concerned with the sorrows of noble Trojan dames, Hecuba, Andromache, Cassandra, just after the fall of Troy. The *Helen* (412 B.C.) turns on the story, made popular by the lyric poet Stesichorus in his 'recantation,' that only a wraith of Helen went to Troy; the real Helen went to Egypt, and was rescued from its king Theoclymenus by a trick of her disguised lord, Menelaus.

41. The *Phoenissae* (411 B.C.) deals with the war levied against Thebes by the Argives, in support of the claim of Polyneices to the throne against that of his brother Eteocles. The chorus consists of 'Phoenician Maidens,' brought from Tyre to serve in the temple of Apollo at Delphi, and detained at Thebes by the outbreak of the war; probably Euripides wished to vary from the 'Seven against Thebes' of Aeschylus, in which the chorus is of Theban women. The *Electra* (410 B.C.), on the same theme as the Choephori of Aeschylus and the Electra of Sophocles, well illustrates the poet's manner. His Electra is a reduced gentlewoman, living in the cottage of a worthy man with whom she has gone through the forms of marriage. In the *Orestes* (408 B.C.) Apollo rescues Helen from the sword of Orestes, who has gone mad after murdering his mother.

42. The *Iphigenia at Aulis* and the *Bacchae* were brought out after the poet's death by his son, the younger Euripides. The former shows how Iphigenia, doomed by her father Agamemnon to be sacrificed at Aulis in order that the wind might become

fair for the Greek fleet, was rescued by the goddess Artemis, who carried the maiden off to her temple among the Tauri in the Crimea. In the *Bacchae* ('female Bacchants'), Pentheus, king of Thebes, arrests the disguised god Dionysus, who has brought his wild bacchanal revelry among the Thebans. But the god takes a terrible vengeance. The king is rent in pieces by his own mother Agâvê and her companions, in the frenzy of their bacchant orgies. This wonderful tragedy has all through it a flashing of divine light, a Dionysiac glory of joy or terror, which is sometimes more oriental than Greek. It was composed or finished in Macedonia—in that northern region where the Thracian bacchants were said to have rent Orpheus in pieces; and it has the true fire of their worship. On that summer evening in the Asiatic camp when the gory head of the Roman Crassus was brought to the Parthian general's tent, it was brought to the sound of the verses in which the Agâvê of Euripides vaunts her ghastly trophy.

43. The *Cyclops* is the only specimen of a satyr-drama that we have. It turns on the adventure of Odysseus with Polyphêmus, and has a good deal of rollicking buffoonery, but little wit, and is not too short at 700 lines. The *Rhesus*, which used to be attributed to Euripides, is now generally supposed to be by some indifferent poet of the latest Attic time. Its theme is the midnight raid of Odysseus and Diomede on the tents of the Thracian Rhesus at Troy.

44. Euripides has been the most generally popular of the three tragedians; his homeliness and his unrestrained pathos bring him nearer to every-day life. But in his hands Tragedy loses that ideal beauty which Sophocles had raised to perfection. Euripides cared less to make his play a harmonious whole. He relied more on particular scenes or situations. As his drama was less artistically planned, he was obliged to help it out by mechanical devices. One of these was a '*prologue*' in the special sense—a long set speech at the opening of the piece, in which the actor gives a sketch of the facts which it is needful for the

spectators to know. Another was the 'god from a machine,'—a deity brought in suddenly to cut some knot in the action. 'Sad Electra's poet,' as Milton called him, excelled in pathetic power, and especially in expressing the sorrow or tenderness of women; though he never drew a woman so noble or so nobly tender as the Antigone of Sophocles. Kings and heroes in rags or on crutches, heroes and heroines bathed in tears, lamentations long drawn out, abound in his plays; and his skill in working on the feelings led Aristotle to call him, not, indeed, the greatest dramatist, but 'the most tragic' of the poets. The songs of the Chorus in Euripides have less to do with the action than in Aeschylus or Sophocles; and he made much use of lyric *menodies,* plaintive or sentimental airs for one voice.

45. He was deeply influenced by Anaxagoras, who taught that *Intelligence* (*nous*) is the supreme principle by which matter has been reduced to order. Euripides is sometimes inclined to identify Zeus with this Intelligence. Sometimes he leans to pantheism, and makes Zeus 'the vast aether that holds earth in his soft embrace.' But on one point he is clear: 'If the gods do anything base, they are not gods.' Aristophanes most unjustly said of him, 'he has brought men over to believe that there are no gods.' Euripides was versed in those new studies of rhetoric and logic which the old school hated. He frequently mars his dialogue with rhetorical argument, but it was unfair to accuse him of recommending dishonest casuistry. One of his lines, for instance, was constantly quoted against him: 'My tongue has sworn, but my mind is not bound by the oath.' If, however, we look at the context in the *Hippolytus,* we find the poet's meaning to be that a man is not morally bound by a promise extracted from him on false pretences.

Euripides was a great picturesque dramatist. In the *Bacchae* he has given us a romantic drama of such brilliant fancy as we find in no Greek poet except Aristophanes, and the same quality belongs in large measure to the *Ion.* With this gift, and with his tender pathos, he can never lose his charm for the modern world.

46. Aeschylus first gained the tragic prize in 484, Sophocles in 468, Euripides in 442. The great tragic art of Athens was completely developed in less than 50 years. Similarly, in England, the space between Marlowe's *Tamburlaine* in 1587 and Ford's *Perkin Warbeck* in 1634 saw the whole of a great dramatic literature created. But, apart from the rapidity of the growth, there are two things which distinguish Athenian drama—its originality, and its marvellous fertility. Drama has arisen spontaneously elsewhere, and not among Indo-Europeans alone. The Chinese did not borrow their drama. The cousins of the Greeks in India created drama of high merit. But **the Greeks of Attica were the first people who made drama a complete and beautiful work of art.** And the 31 tragedies which have been saved to us are but a fraction of a vast literature. Many of the best plays that we have were vanquished by rivals of which the very names are lost. There must have been many tragic poets who, in the estimation of their contemporaries, were nearly on a par with the great three; Agathon, for instance, the friend of Socrates and Plato, probably was so.

47. **Comedy** was twin-born with Tragedy; it sprang from the same worship of Dionysus; but it was later in reaching its maturity. A worship founded on the personification of natural forces necessarily consecrates mirth as well as mourning, for it consists in the impassioned observation of contrasts. If the darkening of the year, the withering of the leaves, the freezing of the earth, claim a sympathetic sorrow, then a sympathetic joy must welcome the larger light of spring, the sprouting of leaves, the ground newly clad with grass and flowers. In Greek worship mysterious awe and daring jest were often neighbours; but in no worship were they nearer to each other than in that of Dionysus. Frolicsome banter, the outbreak of animal spirits that have been repressed, fitly greet the returning sunshine of the god's fortune as it breaks through the passing cloud.

48. '*Comedy,*' 'the song of the village,' carries us back to the gay vintage feast which the country people kept with feasting

and dancing, with song and jest. The graver hymns sung at such festivals were taken up, we saw, by Arion, arranged artistically for a regular chorus, and thus made the germ of Tragedy. The light, humorous songs—the pleasantry and burlesque—were long left to be extemporised by the people. But these, too, came to be set for a regular chorus, holding a dialogue with an actor on the stage. And here, too, the first step was taken by the Dorians. But the Dorians, who had a turn for broad drollery and homely satire, went a step further in Comedy than in Tragedy. They dramatised the dialogue of 'comic' chorus and actor into short farces. SUSARION, who exhibited such farces in Attica about 580 B.C., was a Dorian of Megara; and it is noteworthy that in later days the Sicilian Megara, a colony of its namesake in Greece Proper, was the birthplace of the comic poet EPICHARMUS (450 B.C.). There was a recognised type of *Megarian* farce. A comic writer of about 480 B.C. says that he disdains to make his comedy Megarian; and Aristophanes himself deprecates a joke stolen from Megara. These Megarian farces—like those of the lively Sicilians—probably abounded in broad fun, which the Athenian sense of humour would have found tiresome. After Susarion, we hear of no considerable comic poet till the Attic CHIONIDES, about 488 B.C.

49. **Attic Comedy**, in its artistic form, began about 470 B.C. Aristophanes names MAGNES as the earliest of his predecessors, and describes how, with all his versatility, he failed to keep the favour of the fickle crowd. The first great name is **Cratînus** (448 B.C.), who 'was borne on a full tide of praise.' CRATES, nearly his contemporary, pleased Athens by his glowing fancy and his 'most dainty conceits.' **Eupolis**, whose first play was brought out in 429 B.C., directed a satire as bitter, if not as witty, as that of his rival Aristophanes against the vices of the day. One of his best-known pieces was a savage attack on a profligate set of which Alcibiades was the centre.

50. **Aristophanes** was probably born about 448 B.C. His father Philippus owned property in Aegina; and there is no

reason to doubt the son's claim to Athenian citizenship, though his enemy, the demagogue Cleon, seems to have indicted him more than once as a usurper of civic rights. He tells us himself how fully he realised that careful preparation was needful for a poet who wished to keep the favour of Athens. He had seen his predecessors suffer from the people's inconstancy. It was his maxim that one should serve an apprenticeship as both oarsman and steersman before one took command of a ship. But when, at the early age of twenty-one, he did come forward, he kept his place.

For nearly 40 years Aristophanes was the great burlesque critic of Athenian life, political, intellectual, moral and social. We have only 11 of the 54 comedies which he is said to have written, and these fall into three groups.

51. The plays of the **first group** use unrestricted licence of satire. His career began with two plays now lost; the *Banqueters* (427 B.C.), a contrast between the Old School and the New; the *Babylonians* (426 B.C.), a satire on the treatment of the allies of Athens by the demagogues. Then came our *Acharnians* (425 B.C.)—a plea for the peace-party against the war-party, the latter being represented by the men of Acharnae, whose vineyards have been laid waste by the Peloponnesians. In the *Knights* (424 B.C.) he continues his attack, begun in the 'Babylonians,' on the demagogue Cleon. No mask-maker could be found to take the risk of caricaturing Cleon; 'but you will know him,' says the poet,—'the house is clever.' In the *Clouds* (423 B.C.) he attacks the new spirit of inquiry and culture. Physical philosophers like Anaxagoras, teachers of rhetoric like Protagoras, are classed together under the common name of 'sophist;' and Socrates is taken as the type of the whole tendency. In the *Wasps* (422 B.C.), on which Racine founded *Les Plaideurs*, we are shown how the demagogues treat their deluded allies, the citizens who form the large juries in the law-courts. The *Peace* (421 B.C.) resumes the purpose of the 'Acharnians.' Trygaeus, a distressed Athenian, flies up to heaven on a beetle,

and there finds the gods engaged in pounding the Greek States in a mortar. He succeeds in liberating the goddess Peace from her prison, and winning her blessings for Greece.

52. The plays of the second group differ from those of the first in the greater reserve with which political satire is employed. In the *Birds* (414 B.C.), two enterprising Athenians persuade the birds to build a cloud-city by which the gods are cut off from men, and so brought to terms. It is a medley of sportive fancies, full of allusions to the Athenian follies of the day, and especially to the expedition against Sicily. The *Lysistrata* appeared just before, the *Thesmophoriazusae* just after, the reign of terror established by the Four Hundred in 411 B.C. In the former, the women seize the government, with a view to ending the Peloponnesian War. In the latter, Euripides is tried and condemned at the female festival of the Thesmophoria. The *Frogs* (405 B.C.) came out when Athens was exhausted by her last effort in the war,—a few months before her final defeat at Aegospotami. Euripides and Sophocles had both recently died. Euripides and Aeschylus are represented contending for the tragic prize among the dead, and the prize is won by Aeschylus.

53. The **third group** consists of two plays, in which the old strain of personal satire has almost disappeared. The *Ecclesiazusae* (392 B.C.) shows how the 'Women in parliament' contrived to frame a new constitution. The *Plutus* (388 B.C.) relates how eye-sight was restored to the god of wealth, who proceeds to enrich the good and beggar the wicked.

54. **Spirit of the Great Attic Comedy.** Attic Comedy, as we have it in Aristophanes, is a public commentary on the every-day life of Athens, in great things and small. Politics and society, statesmen and private persons, are criticised with unsparing freedom. The satire is unscrupulously *personal.* Old Athens knew no respect for private life when it seemed to be for the good of the city that the vices of a citizen should be lashed. At the carnival of Dionysus the poet had, as it were, a public charter to speak his whole mind to the citizens. Such a power

was sure to be sometimes abused, and the license of Comedy was more than once restrained by legal enactment. The special weapon of the old Attic Comedy was its power of holding up a man or a policy to admiration or ridicule before some 20,000 legislators. Broad as the farce might be, the effect on public opinion was often, probably, very great.

55. **The Chorus in Comedy** consisted, not of 12 or 15 persons as in Tragedy, but usually of 24. They were dressed as fantastically as the figures in a modern pantomine or extravaganza. Thus, in the '*Wasps*,' the Chorus were dressed to look as much as possible like huge wasps, pinched at the waist and armed with skewers for stings; in the *Birds*, the Choruses were gorgeously arrayed in 24 different kinds of plumage. This burlesque element was quite in keeping with the frolic of a Dionysiac festival. At some point suited for a pause in the action—usually towards the middle of the play—the Chorus faced round towards the spectators, drawing nearer to them. This was their **parabasis**, or 'coming forward' to the house—a name given especially to the *address* which the leader of the chorus then spoke, setting forth the merits or grievances of the poet, or his views on public affairs. These lines from the *Peace*[2] will give a notion of the form and tone. Aristophanes is claiming to have elevated Comedy:

> It was he that indignantly swept from the stage the paltry ignoble device
> Of a Heracles needy and seedy and greedy, a vagabond sturdy and stout,
> Now baking his bread, now swindling instead, now beaten and battered about.
> And freedom he gave to the lacrimose slave who was wont with a howl to rush in,
> And all for the sake of a joke which they make on the wounds that disfigure his skin,...
> Such vulgar contemptible lumber at once he bade from the drama depart,
> And then, like an edifice stately and grand, he raised and ennobled the Art.

This interlude of the parabasis could be left out when it did not suit the poet to speak his mind freely. Thus the *Lysistrata*—on the eve of the Revolution of the Four Hundred—has no parabasis. And as Comedy lost its old audacity of political and personal satire, the parabasis was dropped altogether. There is none in the two latest plays of Aristophanes, the *Ecclesiazusae* and the *Plutus*. In the *Plutus*, indeed, the Chorus has no choral songs, but merely takes part in the dialogue.

56. Aristophanes was not only a great satirist but a great poet. His comedies unite elements which meet nowhere else in literature. There is a play of fancy as extravagant as in a modern burlesque; the whole world is turned topsy-turvy; gods and mortals alike are whirled through the motley riot of one great carnival. There is a humour as delicate, a literary satire as keen, as the most exquisite wit could offer to the most subtle appreciation. And there are lyric strains of a wild woodland sweetness hardly to be matched save in Shakespeare. Aristophanes clung to the old traditions of Athens with a sort of jovial, unreasoning toryism. Demagogues, philosophers, rhetoricians were his abomination. His ideal was the plain, sturdy citizen of the good old school who beat the Persians at Marathon. He claims for himself, and justly, that he is outspoken on the side of virtue against vice. But his personal judgments must be taken with reserve. Thus, though an admirable critic, he was unfair to the poet Euripides; and he exaggerated the case against his enemy, Cleon.

57. **'Old,' 'Middle,' 'New' Comedy.** The Old, or great political, Comedy of Athens, lasted from about 470 to 390 B.C., culminating and beginning to decline with Aristophanes. The Middle Comedy, from about 390 to 320 B.C., marked the period of transition from political to purely social Comedy. It has no longer the old boldness of fancy or bitterness of attack; philosophy and literature are criticised rather than politics; the element of choral music disappears. Among its poets were ANTIPHANES, reputed the author of 260 pieces, and ALEXIS, of

245; also two sons of Aristophanes, ARÂROS and PHILIPPUS. The **New** Comedy, vigorous from about 320 to 250 B.C., was more like our modern Comedy of manners. The stock characters were such as the stern or weak father, the son whose follies are seconded by a slave or a hungry parasite, the pettifogger, active in stirring up lawsuits, and the gasconading soldier of fortune. Such poets as MENANDER, PHILÊMON and DIPHILUS, appear to have excelled in fine delineation of character. The Roman dramatists imitated them. Julius Caesar called Terence 'a half Menander'—having his elegance of style, but not his comic force. In speaking of 'Old,' 'Middle,' 'New' Comedy, we must always remember that they are merely successive phases of **one unbroken development**, which followed necessarily on the decay and final extinction of the old political life at Athens.

Notes

1. 18, including the *Cyclops.*
2. Translated by Mr Rogers.

5

The Beginnings of Prose—History

Early Ionian prose-writers, 550—450 B.C. Herodotus, (b. 484, d. 428 B.C., or later). Thucydides, (b. 471, d. about 400 B.C.), Xenophon, (b. about 431, d. 354 B.C.).

1. Greek Poetry had matured its last great form in the Attic drama before a true prose literature had begun. The late origin of literary prose in Greece is partly explained by the paramount interest which Epic poetry so long secured for the legends of the heroic past, and by the ease with which elegiac or iambic verse subsequently responded to all the needs of expression felt by a cultivated and thoughtful man. In part it is also due to the fact that Greece was broken up into small States, each busied with its own affairs and its own traditions. Hence there was no such national demand for a national record as might have hastened the literary use of prose. Homer was the national history. The Persian Wars first gave to the Greeks a great theme of common interest.

The delay in the rise of prose literature was in one way a gain. So much the wider and firmer became that poetical basis on which the culture of the Greeks reposed. The spiritual elevation, the true liberality, the nobleness of conception which belonged to the best Greek character are in some measure fruits of that long sovereignty which great poetry had held over the race.

2. **Earliest Prose-Writers.** Literary prose, like artistic poetry, began in Ionia. About 550 B.C. PHERECYDES of Syros (who must be distinguished from the annalist Pherecydes of

Leros, 450 B.C.) set forth his speculative theology in what is usually regarded as the earliest Greek prose. The Ionian philosophers ANAXIMENES and ANAXIMANDER also wrote in prose. This earliest prose seems to have been in the form of brief, sententious utterances, either disjointed or roughly strung together, and analogous to the pithy maxims ascribed to the 'wise men' of the same age. Thinkers who desired an artistic form for their thought still preferred verse, as did the Ionian philosophers Xenophanes and Parmenides, and the Sicilian Empedocles in his great poem 'On Nature.'

3. Towards the end of the 6th century B.C. prose began to be used with more freedom by those Ionian writers who were especially called **logographi, 'narrators in prose,'** as opposed to *epopoii,* 'narrators in verse.' These writers had two chief branches of work: (1) They compiled the ancient myths or legends of Greece, and especially the *genealogies* of the great houses. (2) They combined geography with uncritical and fragmentary history in the description of foreign countries, usually after personal travel. Essays in both kinds were often made by the same writer, as by **Hecataeus** of Miletus (500 B.C.), who wrote a *Tour of the Earth,* and also *Genealogies,* in which he showed how he himself had had a god for his sixteenth ancestor. **Hellanicus** of Mitylene (450 B.C.) marks the transition from mere compilation to more careful work. He wrote a history of Attica, of many other places in Greece, and of Egypt, Persia, Phoenicia; and seems to have been among the first who attempted a critical comparison of authorities.

4. **Herodotus**, son of Lyxes, was born in 484 B.C. at Halicarnassus in Caria. This city was Dorian, but had a large Ionian element in its population. The family of Herodotus, a noble one, was probably Dorian; but he may have been familiar with the Ionic dialect from his youth. At the time of his birth the city was governed, under Persia, by Artemisia, the queen who fought so bravely for Xerxes at Salamis. Her grandson and successor Lygdamis put to death Panyâsis, the maternal uncle

of Herodotus,—a man known in literature as one of the restorers of epic poetry. Herodotus, we are told, fled from Lygdamis to the Ionian island of Samos; returned to Halicarnassus after the tyrant had been driven out; but again left his native place, and came to Athens about 446 B.C. Athenian power, art and poetry were then at their height under Pericles. Herodotus came at Athens into a society as variously brilliant as the world has ever seen. He was the intimate friend of the poet Sophocles; and we have the beginning of an ode said to have been addressed to him by Sophocles in 440 B.C.,—the year of the *Antigone,* a play in which Sophocles alluded to a story told by Herodotus in his third book. In 443, probably, Herodotus went to Thurii, a colony founded by Athens on the site of Sybaris in South Italy. He visited Athens again, later than 432, for he saw the Propylaea or colonnaded entrance of the Acropolis, completed in that year. His death, probably at Thurii, is placed by some as early as 428 B.C., since there are signs that he did not live to revise his History; by others, as late as 406 B.C.

5. The travels of Herodotus, made chiefly from Halicarnassus in the earlier half of his life, were extensive. Favoured by his two-fold quality as a Persian subject and a Greek citizen, he traversed almost the whole of the known world, from Ecbatana, Susa and Babylon in the east to South Italy in the west, from the northern shores of the Black Sea to the first cataract of the Nile, an area of about **1700 miles square**. No Greek before him had explored foreign lands so widely or so intelligently.

6. The **History** of Herodotus works up the materials thus collected into an artistic picture of the world, grouped round a central idea. This idea is the great struggle between East and West, between Asiatic and Greek, of which the Persian Wars formed the last chapter. The History falls into two chief parts. The first five books are an introduction, tracing the rise and growth of the Persian power. The last four books relate the Persian invasions of Greece under Darius and Xerxes.

Book I contains the career of Cyrus, founder of the Persian

Empire (560—529 B.C.). Books II and III contain the invasion and conquest of Egypt by Cambyses, his death, and the accession of Darius, with a description of Egypt and the Egyptians. Books IV and V contain the Persian campaigns in Scythia and Thrace, with descriptions of the countries; a Persian expedition to Libya, with notices of that land and its Greek colonists; and the story of the Ionian revolt from 501 to 498 B.C.

Book VI, after concluding the Ionian revolt, relates the first Persian expedition against Greece in 492, and the invasion of 490, repelled at Marathon. Book VII relates the invasion of Xerxes, to the battle of Thermopylae (480 B.C.); Book VIII, the battles of Artemisium and Salamis, and the flight of Xerxes (480); Book IX, the battles of Plataea and Mycale (479), the retreat of the Persian general Mardonius (479 B.C.), and the capture by the Greeks of Sestos on the Hellespont.

7. *The god loves to cut down all towering things...the god suffers none but himself to be haughty. Rash haste ever goes before a fall; but self-restraint brings blessings, not seen at the moment perhaps, yet found out in due time.* These are the words that Herodotus makes the wise Artabanus speak to his nephew, Xerxes, king of Persia, dissuading him from the attack on Greece; but Xerxes answers him with insult. They are the key-note of the History. It is a prose tragedy, which justifies the ways of Heaven to men by showing how sin is punished with ruin. According to the best accounts, says Herodotus, the quarrel between barbarian and Greek began by Phoenician sailors carrying off the maiden Io from Argos. Greeks retaliated by carrying off Europe from Tyre. Then Greeks began wrong anew by taking Medea from Colchis; and next the Phrygian Paris robbed the Spartan king of Helen. The Greeks sacked Troy. Ages passed before a strong champion of Asia arose. And, when he came, his spirit was hateful to Heaven. Xerxes was the type of the man whom the gods love to humble,—the lord of all pleasure, all pomp, all power, one whom men revere as a god and who treats men as slaves. From Susa to the Hellespont, from the Hellespont to the

Gates of Greece, he moves on with his countless host. He is mad with pride. He sends his spoilers against Delphi. But the god himself beats them back. He takes Athens. But dark signs hint that the gods of Athens and Eleusis are against him. And now his cup is full. Salamis—Plataea — Mycale—these three defeats are the three falls which Greece gave to Persia, freedom to slavery, the justice of the gods to mortal pride.

8. The originality of Herodotus fairly entitles him to be called, in one sense, the 'father of History.' He has, of course, some general traits in common with the Ionian writers of his own or an earlier day. Like them, he records myths, though seldom quite uncritically; he describes foreign countries geographically and socially; and he writes in that Ionic dialect which was then the recognised organ of literary prose. He made direct use, too, of some earlier writers, such as Hecataeus and Hellanicus. But no one before him had worked large masses of facts into a symmetrical whole, with unity of plan and thought. He was **the first artist in prose.** As a historian, he fails chiefly by inattention or insensibility to political cause and effect. He will account for a great event merely by some accident which was the immediate occasion of it, without seeking to find any deeper source. And he tells us little or nothing about constitutional change. His charm of style is all the greater for his almost child-like simplicity, and he is one of the most delightful story-tellers. His narrative flows on in what the Greeks called the *running* style, seldom attempting compact *periods.* Often he stops to tell some quaint little story by the way—like that of Hippocleides, a noble suitor for the daughter of the great prince Cleisthenes, who pained his intended father-in-law by dancing before the company, and finally stood upon his head. Cleisthenes, who had hitherto restrained himself, exclaimed,—'Son of Tisandrus, you have danced off the marriage'; but Hippocleides replied, *Hippocleides does not care.* Hence, says Herodotus, our proverb.

9. **Thucydides**, born in 471 B.C., was the son of Olorus, an Athenian citizen. This Olorus was probably grandson of the

Thracian prince Olorus, whose daughter Hegesipylê married Miltiades, the conqueror at Marathon. Thucydides would thus be a younger cousin of the statesman Cimon. He was forty years of age when, the Peloponnesian War began in 431. From its beginning, he tells us, he foresaw that it was destined to be more momentous than any war before it, and watched its course closely, with a view to writing its history. The turning-point of his life came in 424 B.C., the eighth year of the war. He was then in command of an Athenian fleet off the Thracian coast. On this coast, opposite the island of Thasos, Thucydides possessed a property of gold-mines. While Thucydides was at Thasos with his ships, the Spartan general Brasidas surprised Amphipolis on the Strymon, the chief town held by Athens in those parts. It was a terrible disaster. The Athenians deprived Thucydides of his command. There is no ground for charging him with anything so base as the wish to guard his own estate at the cost of his duty. But it seems difficult to excuse him for having been 50 miles from Amphipolis at a time when Brasidas was hovering about it. We do not know that he was banished. But we know that from 423 to 403 he was in exile from Athens. He spent these 20 years partly on his property in Thrace, partly among the Peloponnesians and their allies,—always keeping in mind his great purpose, to write the history of the war. He returned to Athens on the restoration of the democracy in 403 B.C. His death cannot have been later than 396, and may probably be placed about 400. According to a contemporary account, he was assassinated in Thrace; his ashes were brought to Athens, and laid in the tomb of the house of Cimon.

10. The **History** of Thucydides falls into three parts, of which the last is unfinished. 1. The first four Books, with chapters 1—18 of Book V, contain the history of the war from its beginning in 431 to the Peace of Nicias in 421: sometimes called the 'Archidamian War,' from the invasions of Attica led by Archidamus king of Sparta. 2. In Book V (from chapter 19), Books VI and VII, we have the next eight years, comprising that war in the Peloponnesus of which Argos was the centre, and the

Athenian expedition against Sicily. 3. Book VIII begins the third chapter of the struggle, called the Decelean War, from the Spartan occupation of Decelea in Attica (413 B.C.). It would naturally go down to the battle of Aegospotami (405), or the surrender of Athens to Lysander (404). But Book VIII breaks off in the middle of chapter 109, shortly after the great victory of the Athenians (in 411 B.C.) at Cynossêma. Alleged differences of style, and the absence of set speeches, have brought suspicion on the eighth Book; but there can be little doubt that it is the unfinished work of Thucydides.

11. Herodotus was the literary founder of History; Thucydides was **the first philosopher of History**. He seeks not only to give an accurate, concise narrative of events, but also to show the causes from which the events sprang, the political or moral lessons which they convey. Thus he is not content with saying that the Peloponnesian War arose from the disputes between Athens and Corinth about Epidamnus and Potidaea. He goes back beyond these immediate and obvious causes to deeper, more essential causes—the fear which the empire of Athens had spread throughout Greece, and the impulse of Sparta to come forward as the champion of Greek freedom against Athenian aggression. When he has given, in a few bold touches, a picture of the strife between oligarchs and democrats at Corcyra, he analyses the state of political morals out of which the strife arose. A passionless, judicial tone prevails throughout. He seldom awards personal praise or blame. *The absence of romance in my History,* he says, *will perhaps lose it the popular ear. But it will be enough if it is judged useful by those who may desire an accurate knowledge of the past as a clue to that future which, in all human probability, must repeat or resemble the past. It has been composed, not as the exploit of an hour, but as a possession for all time.*

12. And such it truly is; Thucydides has well been called 'the historian of our common humanity, the teacher of abstract political wisdom.' The literary characteristics of his work are

also striking. Much of the closest thought is conveyed in set **speeches**, put into the mouths of the historical persons. Some of these speeches represent the general purport of speeches actually made. Others are altogether the invention of Thucydides. But the thoughts and sentiments are always such as, in the judgment of Thucydides, the particular speaker might have expressed. The longest and most elaborate speech is the *Funeral Oration* spoken by Pericles over those who fell in the first year of the war—a magnificent picture of the Athenian spirit in politics and in social intercourse. Like the other speeches, it is an essay by Thucydides himself in the fashionable rhetoric of the day, which was somewhat stiff, and too fond of verbal contrasts, but capable both of grandeur and of pathos.

13. A greater master of stern pathos than Thucydides never lived, and this is partly because he never says too much. He was not only a political philosopher, but also an artist who felt the tragic force of his story. Thus he fixes our attention on Athens at the summit of her cruelty and insolence—in the massacre at Mêlos—just before he passes to the terrible narrative of her ruin in Sicily. His style has many faults. It is often involved, abrupt, obscure. But no writer has grander bursts of rugged eloquence, or more of that greatness which is given by sustained intensity of noble thought and feeling.

14. **Xenophon**, through his own writings, is better known to us as a man than almost any Greek author. The story that Socrates saved his life at the battle of Delium (424 B.C.) has caused his birth to be dated about 445 B.C. But the story is probably a fiction. From his own words it seems clear that he cannot have been more than about thirty in 401. His brother Gryllus was an Athenian citizen of good position, and gave him a liberal education. He became the disciple of Socrates, whose teaching was the basis of his principles throughout life. In the spring of 401 B.C., at the advice of his Boeotian friend Proxenus, he went to Sardis in Asia Minor, and joined an expedition, including more than 10,000 Greek mercenaries, which the young

Persian prince Cyrus was preparing to lead into Persia, for the purpose of wresting the crown from his elder brother Artaxerxes II.

15. Xenophon has told the story of this expedition in one of the most fascinating books in the world, his **Anabasis**, in seven books. The title means 'a march *up* (*from the coast*)' into the interior, and properly applies only to the first part, as far as the battle at Cunaxa (a name not mentioned by Xenophon, but given by Plutarch) about 50 miles from Babylon, where Cyrus was killed (Sept. 401). The remaining and larger part of the work ought rather to be called *Catabasis,* the march *down* to the sea. Soon after the death of Cyrus, the Persian satrap Tissaphernes treacherously seized five of the Greek generals. The Greeks were now in terrible danger. That night Xenophon—who had not hitherto been either an officer or a private soldier, but simply an 'unattached' volunteer—dreamed that his father's house was set on fire by lightning. What did this portend? That the king of Persia—figured by the King of Heaven—was to destroy them? Or, that, in their dark hour, a great light was to come to them from on high? Xenophon started up, awoke the surviving leaders, and in a midnight council of war, gave them heart, by his plain earnest eloquence, to take measures for the common safety.

16. Next day, formed in a hollow square with the baggage in the centre, they began the Retreat. Moving along the Tigris, past the site of the ancient Nineveh and the modern Mossul, they came into the country of the Carduchi, or Kurds, who, like modern Kurds, rolled down stones on them from the top of their mountain-passes; then through Armenia and Georgia. At last one day—in the fifth month—February, 400 B.C.—Xenophon, who was with the rearguard, heard a great shouting among the men who had reached the top of a hill in front. He thought they saw an enemy. He mounted his horse, and galloped forward with some cavalry. As they came nearer, they could make out the shout: it was '*the sea*! *the sea*!' There, far off, was the silver gleam of the Euxine. After the long, intense strain of

toil and danger, the men burst into tears; like true Greek children of the sea they knew now that they were in sight of home. Two days' march brought them to the coast at *Trapezus*, a Greek city, the modern Trebizond; there they sacrificed to the gods, especially to Zeus the Preserver and Heracles the Guide. This Retreat showed Greece how weak Persia really was, and encouraged the expedition of Alexander. In Xenophon's phrase, they had mocked the Great King at his own doors.

17. From Trebizond the Greeks, now reduced to about 8600, gradually made their way to Byzantium (Constantinople). After two months' service with Seuthes, a Thracian prince, the remnant of 6,000 were incorporated, at Pergamus in the Troad, with the army of the Lacedaemonian general Thimbron, who was making war on the Persian satraps Tissaphernes and Pharnabazus. Xenophon then left them in March, 399 B.C. This was the year in which Socrates was put to death,—a crime by which Xenophon, already unfriendly to the Athenian democracy, was further embittered against Athens. He served in Asia under his favourite hero, the Spartan king Agesilaus, and fought under him against the Athenians and Thebans at the battle of Coronea in 394.

18. Then, if not earlier, he was formally banished from Athens. The Spartans rewarded him with the gift of an estate at Scillus, a village about two miles from Olympia, in Elis, where, with his wife and two sons, he lived a happy country life for about twenty years, busied with writing and hunting. After the great defeat of Sparta at the battle of Leuctra in 371 B.C. he is said to have been driven from Scillus and to have settled at Corinth. We hear that the Athenians revoked his sentence of banishment, perhaps in tribute to the bravery of his son Gryllus, who fell on the Athenian side at Mantinea, in 362 B.C. Xenophon died about 354 B.C.

19. Besides the *Anabasis*—which he did not publish in his own name, but in that of Themistogenes, a Syracusan—his chief historical work is the **Hellenica**, a history of Greece in seven

books, beginning in 410 B.C., soon after the battle of Cynossêma in 411, and ending with the battle of Mantinea in 362 B.C. The first two Books were probably composed not later than 400 B.C., in continuation of the unfinished work of Thucydides, and differ much from the last five books both in expression and in tone of thought. It is a dry history, enlivened occasionally by short speeches or conversations, but disfigured by the author's prejudices in favour of Sparta, and by a jealous idolatry of Agesilaus which makes him keep other men in the background. Xenophon relates the first Theban invasion of the Peloponnesus without telling us that Epameinondas founded Megalopolis and restored Messene; and he relates the revolution at Thebes without naming Pelopidas. Yet, with all its faults, the work is precious as our chief continuous authority for the history of the Spartan and Theban supremacies.

20. In the **Recollections of Socrates** Xenophon seeks to vindicate the teaching of his master from the vulgar charges of impiety or immorality, and to illustrate it by anecdotes of his life and conversation. His Socrates has not the delicate irony of Plato's Socrates, and it may be doubted whether Xenophon always caught the real drift of the master; but the book is interesting, not only because it preserves many genuine traits and sayings, but also as showing how Socrates impressed a thoroughly practical, rather blunt mind. In the Treatise *On Domestic Economy (Oeconomicus)*, Socrates relates how a model Athenian husband had given him his views on the proper way of educating a young wife who, when she married at the age of fifteen, understood nothing but cookery. Nothing is said about intellectual training; but the virtues of a good wife and husband are agreeably drawn. The *Banquet*—written probably before Plato's dialogue of the same name—is an interesting picture of an Athenian supper-party, enlivened partly by a professional juggler's troupe, partly by conversation—especially by the discourse of Socrates on the heavenly and the earthly Love. The *Defence of Socrates* on his trial, which bears Xenophon's name, is probably a scholastic exercise of later date.

21. The **Cyropaedia**, or 'Education of Cyrus,' is a sort of historical romance in eight books, describing how Cyrus, the founder of the Persian Empire (who died in 529 B.C., and who must not be confounded with the young Cyrus of the *Anabasis*, killed in 401 B.C.), was educated, how he distinguished himself as statesman, general and king, and how, on his death-bed, he gave counsel to his sons and ministers. The work is not historically accurate, nor is it a true picture of Persian thought or manners, but rather an encomium on Socratic principles and Spartan practice, in which Cyrus himself—drawn with some touches from the young Cyrus whom Xenophon had known— is half a Socrates and half an Agesilaus. The story of the Assyrian prince Abradates, whose beautiful wife Panthea killed herself when he fell fighting for her chivalrous captor, Cyrus, is the earliest prose love-story in European literature. An instance of the Socratic tone is the story of Cyrus being chastised by his tutor for confirming the act of the big boy with the small coat who had forced the little boy with the large coat to an exchange.

22. The *Hiero* is a dialogue in which Hiero II, tyrant of Syracuse, envies the blessedness of a private station, and the poet Simonides paints the possible beneficence of a despot. The essay *On the Lacedaemonian Polity* commends especially the hardy training of Spartan citizens by the State. The essay *On the Athenian Polity* is not by Xenophon, but was written, with oligarchic sympathies, about 420 B.C. It is thus **the oldest extant specimen of literary Attic prose**. The treatise *On the Revenues of Athens* suggests how they may be enlarged, as by increasing the number of the tax-paying resident aliens, or farming out 10,000 slaves to work the silver-mines at Laurium. It is probably not by Xenophon, but was written about 346 B.C. in the interest of the Athenian party who held that peace with Philip would ensure the commercial prosperity of the city.

23. The essay *On Horsemanship* gives hints on the choice and the care of horses—especially as to hardening the feet (the Greeks did not shoe their horses with iron); and on the difficult

art of mounting (they had no stirrups). The *Hipparchicus*, or 'Cavalry Officer's Manual,' shows the petty scale and crude tactics of warfare. The essay *On Hunting* deals largely with hare-hunting on foot: there is a rather unsportsmanlike eagerness to kill by any means, but also some real interest in the working of the dogs. Xenophon is not a great artist, but an excellent writer of varied information, whose large knowledge of the world usually saves his prejudices from overpowering his common sense. He is **the earliest essayist**; and curious as a partisan of Sparta who owes his distinctive merits to Athens.

24. **Ctesias** of Cnidus, who lived (415—398 B.C.) as physician at the court of Artaxerxes Mnemon, became the Greek founder of oriental history by his works, written in Ionic Greek, on Persia and India. Only fragments remain. The **application of literary rhetoric to history** began in the school of Isocrates, and was best represented by two of his pupils. **Theopompus** (352 B.C.) continued the history of Thucydides to the battle of Cnidus (394 B.C.), and in his *Philippica* made Philip of Macedon the central figure in a picture of Greek civilisation. **Ephorus** wrote a history of Greece from the Return of the Heracleidae to Philip's siege of Perinthus (340 B.C.). Attic history and archaeology were treated in special works called **Atthides** by several writers from CLEIDEMUS (360 B.C.) onwards. The chief *Atthis* of which fragments remain is that of **Philochorus**, who lived about 306—260 B.C., and carried his history down to 262 B.C.

6

Oratory, Philosophical Prose

Oratory. Antiphon (b. 480, d. 411 B.C.) Andocides, flor. 415—390. Lysias, master of the plain style of oratory, flor. 403—381. Isocrates, founder of literary rhetorical prose, (b. 436, d. 338). Isaeus, the master of forensic argument, flor. 390—353. Demosthenes (b. 384, d. 322). His contemporaries: Aeschines, Lycurgus, Hypereides, Deinarchus, Demades.—Decline of oratory begins with Demetrius Phalereus, flor. 318 B.C.

Philosophy. Plato (b. 429, d. 347). Aristotle (b. 384, d. 322). Minor Socratic schools: Megarics, Cynics, Cyrenaics.—Beginning of 3rd century B.C.: Epicureans; Stoics.

1. The development of **Attic prose** is seen most clearly in the history of **Attic oratory**. All the Greek poetry and prose of the earlier classical age was meant, in some measure, to be *heard* as well as *read.* The Greek ear was accustomed to look for musical rhythm and finished expression in prose as well as in verse. Public speaking, too, was cultivated as a fine art. It was indispensable to a citizen who wished to make his mark in the public Assembly, or who had to defend himself before a law-court. Greek audiences criticised the style of a speech much as we criticise the style of a book. Hence oratorical prose had a direct and vital bearing on Attic prose generally.

2. Two chief influences combined to form the earliest style of Attic prose: (1) One was that of the **Sophists**, teachers who undertook to prepare young men for the career of active citizens

by training them to readiness in speech and argument, and who brought in a superficial **logic** and **grammar**. The word 'sophist' ('professor of learning or wisdom') was used almost as vaguely as the phrase 'man of letters,' and could be applied without any bad sense to such a man as Plato. Isocrates accepted the name, though he distinguished himself from 'sophists of the herd.' But the 'sophists,' as a class of teachers, got a bad name partly from plain men of the old school who feared their subtlety, partly from philosophers who despised their shallowness. PROTAGORAS and PRODICUS were two of the chief 'sophists.' (2) The other influence was that of the **Sicilian Rhetoric**. CORAX of Syracuse invented his 'Art of Words' (466 B.C.) to help people in pleading their cases before law-courts; it was developed by his disciple TISIAS, through whom it came to Athens. The Sicilians were a lively people, in some things like the Athenians and in others like the Irish—fond of discussion, quick in repartee, and 'never so wretched that they could not make a joke.'

3. **Gorgias** of Leontini in Sicily was neither a 'sophist' in the proper sense nor a student of rhetoric as an art, but rather an independent cultivator of natural oratory, with a gift for brilliant expression of a poetical and often turgid kind. When he visited Athens in 427 B.C. his florid eloquence became the rage, and was afterwards the first literary inspiration of the orator Isocrates.

4. **Antiphon** (born 480 B.C.), the first in the list of the Ten Attic Orators drawn up by later Greek critics, has much in common with the style of Thucydides, and, with him, represents the early Attic prose. The style is elaborate; it moves with a grave dignity; much weight of meaning is concentrated in single words; and pointed verbal contrasts are frequent. There is a certain rugged grandeur, a stern pathos, a scorn for prettiness or florid ornament, but also a lack of ease, grace, and light movement. Antiphon was the ablest debater and pleader of his day, and in his person the new Rhetoric first appears as a political power at Athens. He took a chief part in organising the Revolution of the Four Hundred, and when they fell, was put to

death by the people (411 B.C.), after defending himself in a masterpiece of eloquence. Of his 15 extant speeches, all relating to trials for homicide, 12 are mere sketches or studies, forming three groups of four each, in which the case for the prosecution is argued alternately with the case for the defence. The chief of the three speeches in real causes is that *On the Murder of Herodes*, a defence of a young Mitylenean charged (about 417 B.C.) with the murder of an Athenian citizen.

5. **Andocides**, born of a good family about 440 B.C., was banished from Athens in 415, on suspicion of having been concerned in a wholesale sacrilege,—the mutilation, in one night, of the images of the god Hermes, which stood before the doors of houses and public buildings. He made unsuccessful application for a pardon, first in 411 B.C., during the reign of the Four Hundred, then, after their fall, in 410, when he addressed the Assembly in the extant speech *On his Return*. From 410 to 403 he lived a roving merchant's life in Sicily, Italy, Greece, Ionia and Cyprus. In 402 the general amnesty allowed him to return to Athens. But in 399 the old charges against him were revived. He defended himself in his extant speech *On the Mysteries* (so called, because it deals partly with a charge that he had violated the Mysteries of Eleusis) and was acquitted. During the Corinthian war he was one of an embassy sent to treat for peace at Sparta, and on his return made his extant speech *On the Peace with Lacedaemon* (390 B.C.), sensibly advising Athens to accept the terms offered by Sparta. The speech *Against Alcibiades* which bears his name is spurious. The chief interest of his work is historical; he is not an artist of style, but he has much natural force and keenness, and excels in vivid description.

6. **Lysias** did a great work for Attic prose, and is, in his own style, one of its most perfect writers. He broke away from the stiff monotony of the old school, and dared to be natural and simple, using the language of daily life, but with perfect purity and grace. His father was a Syracusan, and Lysias, though born at Athens, had not the rights of a citizen. After passing his youth

and early manhood at Thurii in south Italy, he settled at Athens, a wealthy man, in 412 B.C. In 404 he fled from the Thirty Tyrants, who had put his brother Polemarchus to death; and, after the restoration of the Democracy, impeached *Eratosthenes*, one of the Thirty, in the most splendid of his extant speeches (403 B.C.), the only one which we know that he himself spoke at Athens. But in 388 B.C. he addressed the assembled Greeks at Olympia, in a fine speech of which we have a fragment, urging them to unite against the two great foes of Greece—Dionysius, tyrant of Syracuse, in the west, and Persia in the east. The speech *Against Agoratus* (399 B.C.?) was written for the impeachment of an informer who had slandered away the lives of citizens under the Thirty Tyrants. The great majority of our 34 speeches were composed by Lysias for his clients to speak in public or private causes. They show the dramatic skill with which he could adapt his style to the condition and character of the speaker. The old critics regard Lysias as the model of the **plain style** of oratory, which conceals its art, and studies the language of ordinary life, as opposed to the **grand style** represented by Antiphon, and the **middle style** of Isocrates.

7. **Isocrates** differs from the other Greek orators in this, that his discourses were meant to be read rather than spoken. He represents the genius of Attic Greek with less purity of taste than Lysias. But he founded a style of Greek **literary prose**, which, from about 350 B.C., became the standard one for general use. Its chief characteristics are the avoidance of poetical language and of declamation, the use of an ample flowing period, and great smoothness, obtained chiefly by systematic care against allowing a word ending with a vowel to be followed by a word which begins with one. This style, transmitted through the schools of rhetoric, became the basis of Cicero's; modern literary prose has been modelled largely on the Roman; and thus the influence of Isocrates has gone through all literature. He was born in 436 B.C., 5 years before the Peloponnesian war began, and died, aged 98, in 338, just after the battle of Chaeronea. Milton speaks of him as 'the old man eloquent'

whose heart was broken by the news, but the story of his suicide is doubtful.

We have 21 of his discourses. Five are for lawsuits, and belong to his earlier life. The rest are either scholastic-letters, panegyrics, show-pieces, essays on education—or *political*. There are also nine letters to friends, including Philip and Alexander the Great. The ruling idea of his life was that of a war by the united Greeks against Persia. The most brilliant of his writings—the *Panegyricus* (380 B.C.)—on which he is said to have spent ten years—is a plea for such a war, to be led by Athens; and in his *Philippus* he urges Philip to lead it. His *Areopagiticus* (355 B.C.) is a plea for restoring the old moral censorship of the Areopagus; and his discourse (353 B.C.) *On the Exchange of Properties* (so called from the fiction of a law-suit on which it is based) is a defence of his 'philosophy,' or political culture founded on literary rhetoric. The *Encomium on Helen* has much beauty. The *Letter to Demonîcus* is full of precepts which often recall the Socrates of Xenophon.

8. **Isaeus**, born about 420 B.C., has left 11 speeches in will-cases, ranging in date from about 390 (oration V) to 353 B.C. (oration VII). An Athenian could not disinherit his son, nor could he separate his estate from his daughter, though he could choose the person whom she was to marry. If childless, he could divert his estate from the next of kin by *adopting*, either during his life or by testament, an Athenian citizen as his son and heir. The speeches of Isaeus throw a most interesting light on the relations of Attic family life. Their style (best seen in the 8th speech) marks a stage in the development of oratorical prose, the transition from the 'plain' style of Lysias to that full technical mastery which reaches its summit in Demosthenes. Isaeus is the first great artist in forensic controversy.

9. **Demosthenes**, born in 384 B.C. and left an orphan in childhood, studied with Isaeus before, in 363—2, he prosecuted Aphobus and Onêtor, the guardians who had wasted his property; and his speeches against them show that he had

caught the master's secret of close, vigorous argument. He worked hard to make himself a good speaker; we are told how he put pebbles in his mouth and declaimed by the loud sea-waves or while he ran up hill, how he wrote out Thucydides eight times, how he was laughed down by the Assembly and comforted by an actor who found him moping about the harbour-town. Not industry, however, or genius alone, but a great idea inspiring his whole life, lifted him to heights reached by no other orator of the old world. Athens, he believed, was the natural head of Greece. Athens must win the confidence of all the Greeks in order to guard Greece against internal or external violence. But before Athens can do this, the public spirit of Athenians must be revived.

10. Four **speeches in public prosecutions**—*Against Androtion* (355), *Leptines* (354), *Timocrates* and *Aristocrates* (352)—opened his career with protests against corrupt administration at home. Addressing the Assembly in his speeches *On the Navy Boards* (354), *For Megalopolis* (352) and *For the Rhodians* (351), he warns Athens that she must organise her resources, that she must discountenance the tyranny of Greeks over Greeks, and must everywhere support the cause of Greek freedom against barbarian despotism. The speech (neither finished nor spoken) *Against Meidias* (349)—who had assaulted Demosthenes in public—shows what bitter enmity the young reformer had provoked.

11. As Philip of Macedon gradually stretched his power along the coasts of Thrace and Thessaly, Demosthenes saw more and more clearly that this crafty king in the North was the great danger which threatened the disunited Greek cities. His nine **speeches against Philip** form two groups. (1) The *First Philippic* (351 B.C.) urges that a force should be sent to the coasts of Thrace, and that citizens should serve in person. The three, orations for *Olynthus* (349—8) plead the cause of the great city, which, with its confederacy of 32 towns, Philip destroyed in 348. So far, Philip had been a foreign foe. But in

346 he became a Greek power by admission to the Amphictyonic Council. (2) The speeches of the second group—which have to reckon with a more definite Macedonian party within Greece itself—are, the speech *On the Peace* (346), The *Second Philippic* (344), *On the Embassy* (343), *On the Chersonese* and the *Third Philippic* (341). Move by move the Macedonian game was explained by Demosthenes. At the last moment he won Byzantium back to the Athenian alliance, and prevailed on Thebes to join Athens in making a last, but vain, stand at Chaeronea (338).

12. In 336 B.C. Ctesiphon proposed that Demosthenes should receive a golden wreath of honour from the State. The orator Aeschines raised legal objections, but was defeated when the case was tried, and left Athens. At the trial (330 B.C.) Demosthenes made a splendid defence of his past policy in the greatest oration of the old world, the speech. *On the Crown. If the event had been manifest to the whole world beforehand,* he said, *not even then ought Athens to have forsaken this course, if Athens had any regard for her glory, or for her past, or for the ages to come.* In 322—when the rising of the Greeks in the Lamian War, after Alexander's death, had been crushed—Demosthenes took poison to avoid falling into the hands of the Macedonians.

13. Demosthenes is the greatest master of Greek prose. He combines all the best elements in earlier styles, and blends them in new harmonies. Some of his **speeches for private law-suits**, written in the midst of his public career, show how this unapproached artist of political eloquence could at the same time equal or surpass Lysias and Isaeus in their own field. Of our 32 private speeches, only 11 are probably genuine, *viz.* the four against *Aphobus* and *Onêtor*; those against *Spudias, Callicles, Pantaenetus, Nausimachus, Boeotus* ('*on the Name*') and *Canon*; with that *For Phormio.* Firm grasp of facts, sparing use of ornament, sincerity and sustained intensity, are the characteristics which first strike a modern reader in the orations

of Demosthenes. We can no longer feel all the delicate touches of that exquisite skill which made them, to the ancients, such marvellous works of art, and which led detractors to reproach them with excess of elaboration. But we can feel, at least, the orator's splendid mastery of every tone which the Greek language could yield, the intellectual greatness of the statesman, the moral greatness of the patriot who warned his people of the impending blow and comforted them when it had fallen.

14. **Aeschines**, born in 389, or five years before Demosthenes, was a tragic actor and a clerk to the Assembly before he came forward, about 348, as a public speaker. His natural eloquence, fluent, vehement, and often splendid, was set off by a fine person and voice, which the stage had taught him to make effective. In 346 he was twice an envoy to Philip. His speech *Against Timarchus* (345) arraigns this man—who was about to prosecute him for breach of trust on the embassy—as disqualified to speak in the Assembly on account of a vicious life: his speech *On the Embassy* (343), in reply to his former colleague Demosthenes, gained him a narrow acquittal. After the failure of his speech *Against Ctesiphon* (330)—an elaborate attack on the whole life of Demosthenes—he withdrew to Rhodes. The genius shown in his eloquence is marred by the want of earnestness and moral nobleness.

15. **Lycurgus**, of a noble priestly family, steward of the Treasury from 338 to 326, is represented only by his oration *Against Leocrates* (332 B.C.), who had fled from Athens just after the battle of Chaeronea, and who is here indicted for treason in a speech full of lofty indignation, a solemn protest on behalf of public spirit, in which a strain of the old style of Antiphon is blended with the luxuriance of Isocrates.

16. From **Hypereides** we have a speech, nearly complete, *For Euxenippus* (about 330 B.C.), interesting as showing the public belief in the dreams sent by a god to those who slept in his temple; fragments of a *Funeral Oration* on Leosthenes and the comrades who fell with him in the Lamian war (322 B.C.); of

a speech spoken by Hypereides *Against Demosthenes* in 324, when the latter was accused of having taken bribes from Alexander's treasurer Harpalus; and of a speech *For Lycophron* (earlier than 349 B.C.), when Lycurgus was accuser. All these were recovered, between 1847 and 1856, from papyri found in Egypt. Hypereides joined fire and pathos to exquisite wit and grace, and was preferred by some to Demosthenes himself.

17. **Deinarchus**, a Corinthian by birth, the last in the canon of the Ten Attic Orators, has left three speeches, *Against Demosthenes, Aristogeiton* and *Philocles,* written when they were accused of taking bribes from Harpalus in 324 B.C. He was mainly a coarse imitator of Demosthenes, and far inferior, probably, to **Demades**, an orator on the Macedonian side at Athens, from whom there remain a few scanty fragments. **Demetrius of Phalerum**, a pupil of Aristotle, then prepared the decline of Attic oratory in his elegantly luxuriant style, 'preferring his own sweetness to the weight and dignity of his predecessors.'

18. While styles for History and Oratory were thus shaped, Philosophy also found an Attic voice. The **Dialogues of Plato**, apart from their scientific character, are masterpieces of literary genius. Pericles died in the autumn of 429 B.C.; Plato was born in the summer of the same year. The family of his father Ariston was noble, tracing its legendary descent up to Codrus, the last king of Athens. From about the age of twenty Plato was acquainted with Socrates, and he was thirty when his master was put to death in 399. Plato then left Athens for a time, and, after some stay at Megara with Eucleides (not the geometer), is said to have visited Cyrene and Egypt. The words may still be read on the wall of a temple by the Nile, in which a Greek traveller of old days has written that he came there 'many years after the divine Plato.'

In 395 B.C. Plato returned to Athens. Dion, brother-in-law of Dionysius I of Syracuse, met Plato in Italy in 389, and persuaded him to visit the tyrant's court. Plato, having stung Dionysius by his discourse, was delivered to the Spartan envoy

Pollis, who happened to be at Syracuse, and was by him sold as a slave in the market at Aegina; but was redeemed by a friend and restored to Athens. After the death of Dionysius I, Plato twice visited his son Dionysius II at Syracuse: but, though he did not again suffer personal wrong, he found that he could effect no good, and he saw the rule of a sensual despot as he had pictured it in his *Republic.* About 386 B.C. he had begun to teach in the *Academy*—(so called from the hero Acadêmus)—a gymnasium with an olive-grove on the outskirts of Athens, near which Plato had a house and garden. He died in 347 B.C., aged 82.

19. The Greeks were the first people who clearly separated philosophy from theology. The first definite philosophical inquiries in Greece began in the 6th century B.C., about the same time as the rise of Buddhism in the East. Hitherto Greeks had been content to *personify* natural agencies. Now they began to ask, What *are* these agencies? Cannot these agencies be reduced to one or more elementary principles? As one attempt after another failed, thinkers began to ask—'How do we get our knowledge of outward things? and how far can we really know anything at all?'

20. Then **Socrates** came, and saw that, to begin with, we must have a better *method* of search. Let us examine ourselves first of all, and find out, if we can, what we really know and what we only seem to know. For instance,—What is a statesman? 'A statesman is a man like Pericles.' But if Pericles is tall and eloquent, must all statesmen be so? Let us try and separate those qualities which belong to *all* statesmen from those which may be present in one statesman and absent from another. When we have done this, we know a statesman in his *essence.* We have got a *conception* of a statesman. And in this search it will be good to question other people, and see if they can help us. But what sort of subjects is it best worth-while to investigate in this way? The nature of the sun, moon and stars, the causes of eclipses and earthquakes? 'No,' said Socrates: 'there is

something that I want to know *first*; I want to know how I, as a man, ought to live and act.' So Socrates made philosophy **ethical**.

21. But, with all our struggles to reach clear conceptions, how can we be sure that it is even possible for us ever to get a glimpse of the very truth? **Plato** offered an answer. Everything that we in this world can perceive, Plato said, is a mere copy or image of a perfect original, which exists in a world above us. For instance, when we have formed our conception of a statesman, we have not merely made an abstract definition; we have got a little nearer—if we have reasoned rightly—to seeing that which really exists. In a world above this, there *is* a perfect statesman, just as there is a perfect tree, a perfect chair, perfect courage. It is this perfect archetype which really exists; the earthly copy only seems to exist. This is the **Theory of Ideas** (from the Greek word '*idĕa*,' 'aspect,' 'form'), that is, the theory of perfect forms or archetypes. And everything that our souls can perceive is good, true or beautiful, according as it resembles the supreme form or 'idea' of all, **the idea of Good**.

22. But as the earthly copies are usually poor, faint copies, how can they give the human soul any notion of their perfect originals? They could not, Plato answers, if the soul, before coming into our body, had not had glimpses of those originals. The soul has forgotten much of that vision. But it has not forgotten all. Even the faint image, like a bad portrait, can serve to *remind* the soul, if only it strives to recollect, and does not allow the base passions to disturb it. This is Plato's doctrine of **Recollection** (*anamnêsis*). Much of the language in Wordsworth's 'Ode on Intimations of Immortality from Recollections of Early Childhood' might almost pass for Plato's. 'Not in entire forgetfulness' have our souls come hither:

> Hence in a season of calm weather,
> Though inland far we be,
> Our souls have sight of that immortal sea
> Which brought us hither,
> Can in a moment travel thither,

And see the children sport upon the shore,
And hear the mighty waters rolling evermore.

23. Now the human soul naturally *loves* the perfect forms of goodness, truth and beauty when it beholds them; but this **love** (erôs) may be quickened or extinguished by education. Therefore it is important that every human being should be so educated as to quicken that love. And therefore, in a perfect society, the education of all the citizens would be regulated by those who are themselves already in love with the perfect forms; and everything that seems likely to deaden that love would be shut out at any cost. Such a State Plato has sketched in his **Republic,**— the literary original of works so different as St Augustine's *City of God,* Sir Thomas More's *Utopia* (*i.e.* No-land), and Bacon's *New Atlantis.* In his *Laws* he traces many details of an ideal code; thus the city is to be just 9 miles from the sea; the number of citizens is to be just 5040; all traders are to be foreigners; and no citizen under forty years of age is to travel.

24. We have altogether 42 Dialogues under Plato's name, of which about 25 are probably genuine. Philosophic dialogue had been written, before Plato, by the Socratic Alexamenus of Teos, and probably by Zeno of Elea and others. But Plato was the first who raised it to an artistic form. The earliest dialogues, composed either before or shortly after the death of Socrates in 399 B.C., trace the essential characteristics of Platonic method, and illustrate the general spirit of the Socratic teaching in contrast with the teaching of the Sophists. Plato's dramatic power and humour are well shown in the dialogues of this period which introduce pompous or rhetorical sophists; such are the *Protagoras* and the *Euthydêmus.*

25. Soon after his return to Athens in 395 B.C. he published the *Gorgias,* which may be regarded as intimating to the Athenian world that he renounces a political career. The first sketch of the *Republic,* suggesting additional reasons, for such a decision, may have followed at no long interval. In a series of dialogues, beginning perhaps with the *Theaetêtus,* and including the

Sophistes, Politicus, Parmenides, he gradually worked out principles by strict discussion. The *Phaedrus,* composed probably after his first visit to Sicily in 389 B.C., and when he was commencing to teach in the Academy, is related to the *Gorgias* as a mature and amended re-statement, with developments, of the views there traced in outline. Later dialogues, such as the *Symposium, Phaedo, Philêbus,* and the *Republic* in its final form as we have it, show the influence of the school of Pythagoras, which applied a doctrine of mystic numbers to the theory of real existence, and with which Plato became conversant during his travels, especially in Southern Italy.

26. Several dialogues of the earlier time raise questions to which they give no formal answers; they merely hint the direction in which an answer is to be sought. Such are sometimes called *dialogues of search.* Thus the *Lysis* asks, 'What is Friendship?' the *Charmides,* 'What is Temperance?' the *Laches,* 'What is Courage?' the *Theaetêtus,* 'What is Knowledge?' On the other hand, some of the latest dialogues are *didactic,* helping to build up a definite doctrine,—political, as the *Republic and Laws,* or cosmical, as the *Timaeus* and *Critias.*

27. Plato's **style** is on the borderland between poetry and prose; it has exquisite conversational ease and grace; it has also bursts of soaring eloquence, when we seem to be listening to the words of one who is actually looking on some glorious vision. Some of the finest passages occur in the stories or **myths** which occasionally serve to relieve or vary the dialogue; such as the chariot of the soul, in the *Phaedrus*; the world above our own, and the judgment of the dead (*Gorgias* and *Phaedo*); the man Er's visit to the place of departed souls (*Republic*); the creation of man (*Timaeus*); the Island of Atlantis (*Critias*).

28. No heathen taught a purer conception of God than Plato did: in his ideal State he would have no legends told save such as declare that God is good, and the author of good only: the choruses of children, youths and men shall sing to the young and tender souls of children that the life which the gods deem

the happiest is the holiest: and the perfection of man's nature, Plato held, is to bring himself as far as he can into harmony with God. **Philo**, an Alexandrian Jew (20 A.D.), first blended Plato's doctrines with Judaism; and out of this grew in the 3rd century A.D. the mystical school of **Neoplatonism**, teaching that the soul must be purged from the taint of the senses till it can hold direct communion, through the *Ideas*, with God, from whom they emanate.

29. **Aristotle**, son of the physician Nicomachus, was born in 384 B.C. at Stageira, on the gulf of Strymon near Mount Athos in Thrace. His family belonged to a clan tracing descent from the mythical physician *Asclepius* (Aesculapius). In Asclepiad families, we are told, the boys were regularly taught dissection. Aristotle's interest in physical science might thus have been roused in boyhood; but passages in his writings have been thought to indicate that he was at least no practised dissector. His life falls into three chapters.

(i) In 367 B.C., his father being dead, he was sent to Athens by his guardian, Proxenus of Atarneus, and became one of Plato's most distinguished pupils,— 'the mind,' as Plato said, of the school. Plato died in 347, and was succeeded at the head of the Academy by his nephew Speusippus. (2) Aristotle, aged 37, then went to Atarneus in Mysia, of which his former fellow-student Hermeias was now ruler. Hermeias fell a victim to Persian treachery in 344. Aristotle then passed two years at Mitylene. In 342 he was invited by Philip of Macedon to be tutor to Alexander, then a boy of fourteen. In 336 Philip died; Alexander became king; and Aristotle settled at Athens. (3) At Athens, about 334 B.C., he began composing that series of great works which he carried on, without a break, to his death in 322: teaching also in the *Lyceum*, an enclosure with temple and grounds sacred to the Lycean Apollo. From its covered *walks* (*peripatoi*), his school were called the **Peripatetics**.

Alexander died in 323. Athenian jealousies against Aristotle now broke out. He was accused of 'impiety'; but withdrew, before trial, to Chalcis in Euboea. There he died, rather suddenly, in 322 B.C., aged sixty-two; thus closing his life, as he had begun it, in the same year with Demosthenes. We are told by writers who were not inclined to be complimentary that Aristotle had small eyes, thin legs, and a lisp, that he was attentive to his dress, and that his table was luxurious: from which it may be inferred that he did not give any very strong hold to slander.

30. The fate of Aristotle's writings is the subject of a story which, though not unquestioned, has good authority. He left his manuscripts to his pupil Theophrastus. Theophrastus died in 287, and left them to Neleus. Neleus took them to Scepsis in the Troad, where they were hidden in a vault, to save them from being seized for the Library at Pergamus. About 100 A.D., they were sold by the family to Apellicon, a rich Athenian with a taste for book-collecting. In 86 B.C. Sulla took Athens; Apellicon's library went to Rome; there Tyrannion, Cicero's learned Greek friend, got leave to arrange it; and ultimately an edition of Aristotle's manuscripts was brought out at Rome by Andronîcus of Rhodes. Now, about 220 B.C.—that is, while the papers were still in their vault—a catalogue of Aristotle's writings was made at Alexandria, enumerating some 146 works, not one of which we know except from small fragments. What can these have been? It seems likely that they were in large part Aristotle's lost *Dialogues,* written in his earlier days in imitation of Plato, and praised by Cicero for their 'golden flow,' whereas the style of the extant writings is dry and bald;—partly papers by his pupils, or mere forgeries; altogether a collection of small worth. If this is true, nothing but a chain of lucky chances saved Aristotle's great works, which, for hundreds of years, gave a strong bent to the mind of Europe, and which have had a more direct part in shaping modern thought than any writings of the old world.

31. Aristotle took almost all human knowledge, as it then was, and mapped it out into several provinces or **sciences**, seeking to show **what principles were peculiar to each science, and what questions each had to answer**. Aristotle's whole work,

from beginning to end, was *one continuous work,* of which each part led on to the next, and which made, in his view, one organic whole.

32. He began with the **method** of knowledge, and composed the treatises on the science of reasoning which together form his *Organon,* that is 'Instrument,' of reasoning; treating, in connection with this, the art of *Rhetoric,* that is the art of discovering, in any given case, the available means of persuasion. Aristotle was the first to treat Rhetoric on a scientific system as the popular branch of Dialectic. In another treatise he carried the analysis of *Poetry,* considered as an imitative art, through the Epic and Tragic branches. Then he turned to the **practical sciences** of Ethics and Politics. Next—having dealt with that which most immediately concerns man as a moral agent—he went on to the **physical sciences**; and when he died, he seems to have been at work on what we call *Metaphysics,* and what he sometimes called the **First Philosophy**, which seeks to explore the origin and nature of existence and of knowledge itself.

33. Aristotle's greatest achievement was to found **Logic**, the *science of reasoning.* Socrates and Plato had founded **Dialectic**, the *art of discussion.* Aristotle began by trying to find out some general rules which might be useful in this art of discussion. And, as he went on, he perceived that reasoning might, in itself, be a science. He discovered the **syllogism**. He only twice refers to himself,—once in apologising for differing from Plato about the 'Ideas,' and once in saying that he had made out for himself *the process of syllogising.* He does not use the word 'Logic,' which the Stoics seem to have adopted afterwards. He calls it '*Analytic,*' that is, the art of analysing and dissecting the forms in which we reason. **Deductive** reasoning *leads us down* from a general to a particular statement: *e.g.* all men are mortal; A is a man; therefore he is mortal (deductive syllogism). **Inductive** reasoning *leads us on* from a particular to a general statement: *e.g.* A, B, C, D are swans; they are white; therefore all swans are white (inductive syllogism). But this conclusion will not be true

unless A, B, C, D are a complete catalogue of swans. Aristotle **completed the correct analysis of the deductive process.** But he did not work out the analysis of the inductive process with the same completeness. And the reason why he did not was that, to the end, he was a dialectician rather than a man of science.

34. Aristotle's **Ethics** bear the epithet 'Nicomachean,' probably because his son Nicomachus had something to do with editing them. The *Eudemian Ethics* are not by Aristotle, but are a paraphrase of his views by his disciple Eudêmus. From this work Books V, VI, VII of the 'Nicomachean' Ethics were probably borrowed by their editor, to fill up a gap left by Aristotle, who, after writing Books I—IV, wrote VIII—X. The *Magna Moralia,* or 'Great Ethics,' which go over the same ground, are by some later member of the school. The end of all action, Aristotle says, is *happiness.* Man's happiness consists in the harmonious exercise of his best powers according to their own law of *excellence* or *virtue.* Every particular virtue is a mean between two extremes. The Greeks tended to look at 'right' and 'wrong' as the morally *beautiful* and the morally *ugly;* so that virtue becomes a sublime form of good taste. The chief thing that Aristotle's Ethics did was to show that **virtue is a state of the will,** and not, as previous thinkers had said, a state of the *reason;* and that **habits or states of the will** are formed by often doing the same kind of action. ' Man,' Aristotle said, ' is a social creature'; man, apart from society, would be either a god or a brute. Hence the science of what man ought to do (*Ethics*) is only a branch of the science of organised society (*Politics*); and Aristotle was the first who treated Ethics separately from Politics.

35. In the **Politics** he sketches his *Ideal State,* with a population of citizens perhaps 20,000 in number, of whom each is to be educated by the State, to be a landowner of *moderate* wealth, to be personally known to the rulers,—to håve, in turn, a share in ruling,—and to be free from all but political and military tasks. Slavery, he holds, is essential, in order that citizens may have leisure. No citizen is to be a tradesman or a mechanic:

and no interest is to be taken on money. *Monarchy, Aristocracy,* and a mixed Constitutional Government (*Politeia*) are described, with the three forms into which they respectively degenerate,—*Tyranny, Oligarchy* and *Democracy.* Aristotle's remarks on these, and on revolutions, are often curiously illustrated by the history of the Italian Republics. He has no idea of Representative Government.

36. In his contributions to the **science of life**, or what is now called '**biology**,' Aristotle defines *soul,* or the vital principle, as the essential actuality of an organised body,—a marked advance on the popular view of life as something that could detach itself from the body. In his *Researches about Animals* we have **the earliest book on Natural History**. It has been shown that he notices, or indicates, about 500 species, including about 350 vertebrates. One of his contributions to **mental science** was to bring out clearly some of the laws of association of ideas, which distinguishes the human power of *recollection* from the mere *memory* of other animals.

37. During the first four centuries of the Christian era Aristotle busied a long series of Greek commentators. Then came centuries during which he was known to Western Europe only through Latin versions of some of his minor logical works. And then, at the end of the 12th century, the Arabian scholar Averroes (Ibn Raschid) made the great works of Aristotle known by commentaries which were translated into Latin. Thomas Aquinas caused a new translation into Latin. Thomas Aquinas caused a new translation of Aristotle to be made (1260—1270 A.D.) from the Greek; Dante (1300) hails Aristotle as 'the master of those who know'; Chaucer describes the Oxford student of the 14th century who has 'twenty bookes clothed in blake or red' of Aristotle 'at his beddes hed'; and till the second half of the 16th century his authority was almost supreme. His physical theory of the universe, which was the basis of the Ptolemaic, was not finally displaced by the Copernican before the end of the 17th century. To this day, when men talk of 'mind

and matter,' 'final cause,' 'motive,' 'the end of our aims,' 'faculty,' 'habit,' 'actually,' they are talking the Latinised language of Aristotle.

38. **Theophrastus** of Eresus in Lesbos (374—287 B.C.) succeeded Aristotle at the head of the Lyceum, and followed his master in handling physical as well as moral science. We have from him two botanical works, *Researches about Plants* in nine books, and *Principles of Vegetable Life* in six books, which show him to have been a thorough and acute inquirer; also 30 short, lively sketches of character—such as 'The Flatterer,' 'The Grumbler,' 'The Boastful Man,' 'The Man of Petty Ambition.' These **Characters** were the original models of those sketches which English literature produced in the 17th century, such as Hall's *Characterismes of Vertues and Vices,* Overbury's *Characters or Witty Descriptions of the Properties of Sundry Persons,* and Earle's *Microcosmographie.*

39. The **minor Socratic** schools, as they are sometimes called, were the *Megaric,* founded by Eucleides of Megara, distinguished for criticism of reasoning processes, especially for the invention of logical fallacies or puzzles; the *Cynic,* founded by Antisthenes, placing virtue in renunciation of the natural pleasures, and contempt for the natural decencies, of life; the *Cyrenaic,* founded by Aristippus of Cyrene, who pursued equable pleasure through versatile self-discipline. But the school of the **Academy** founded by Plato, and the **Peripatetic** school founded by Aristotle, held the foremost place till the earlier part of the 3rd century B.C. Two new schools then began to gain ground.

40. **Epicurus** (342—270 B.C.) taught the disciples gathered round him at his house near Athens,—in those pleasure-grounds from which Epicureans are called 'the Philosophers of the Garden'—that man should seek the enjoyment of the hour, undisturbed by fear of gods who regard him not, or of that 'death' which is merely the resolution of the body into such atoms as compose the universe. The school called **Stoic**, from the 'Painted Stoa' or Porch at Athens frequented by its masters,

was founded by Zeno (344—260 B.C.) and developed by his followers Cleanthes and Chrysippus. Virtue, they held, is the only good. Nothing is evil except in so far as it is contrary to virtue. And virtue consists in living *according to Nature,* that is, according to the divine reason in which we participate. Stoicism first showed its full power when it took hold on the congenial Roman mind. But, in its best Roman representatives, it never wholly lost the gentleness of its earlier Greek home; and, under the early or the declining Empire, it became the dominant influence in some of the noblest characters that the heathen world had known.

PART III—THE LITERATURE OF THE DECADENCE

7

FROM ALEXANDER TO AUGUSTUS 300—30 B.C.

I. **The Alexandrian Period: 300—146 B.C.** *Poetry*: Callimachus, Lycophron, 260 B.C. Apollonius Rhodius, 194. Aratus, 270. Nicander, 150. Theocritus, Bion, 270; Moschus their younger contemporary—*Learning and Science*: Zenodotus, 280. Aristophanes, 200. Aristarchus, 156. Apollodorus, 140. Euclid, 300. Eratosthenes, Archimedes, 240.— *History*: Manetho, Berosus, 270.

II. **The Graeco-Roman Period: 146 B.C.—529 A.D.** First part:—From the Roman Conquest of Greece to the end of the Roman Republic, 146—30 B.C. *History*: Polybius, 145 B.C.; Diodorus Siculus, 40 B.C.

1. **Hellenism.** When Philip of Macedon defeated the Greeks at Chaeronea, the Greek cities became really dependent on Macedon. They kept their separate laws, but they had no longer any real power of acting in great matters as they chose. Their free political life was gone. Then came Alexander's conquests in the East, and the sudden break-up of his empire at his death into three chief kingdoms, Macedonia, Asia, Egypt. One great result of his conquests had been the spreading abroad of Greek civilisation. Many cities, such as Antioch and Seleucia, were

founded in Western Asia, inhabited partly by Asiatics and partly by Greeks from various parts. Under the rule of Alexander's Successors these new cities in Asia could not have the true life of the old Greek cities, of which the soul was political independence. But in outward things they were Greek. Greek was the language generally spoken. Greek books were read and written. There were Greek temples, statues, baths, porticoes, theatres. **This civilisation, Greek in its general character, but pervading people not exclusively Greek by race**, is properly called **Hellenism**, which means,—not '*being* Hellenes' or Greeks, but—'doing *like* Hellenes'; and as the adjective answering to *Hellas* is *Hellenic,* so the adjective answering to Hellenism is **Hellenistic**.

2. All the great Hellenic poetry and prose had its spring in a spontaneous impulse of the author, who wished to say to his fellow-citizens that which he felt was good and worthy to be heard. And the people tried his work, not by the arbitrary rules of a school or a clique, but by the standard of real experiences, and by a feeling for beauty which had become instinctive through the graciousness of their daily surroundings. The poet of the *Iliad* sang of legends which were a living joy to all who heard them, even as to himself. Simonides and Pindar,—Aeschylus, Sophocles and Euripides,—Herodotus, Thucydides,—all these were creative artists, whose efforts were quickened by the healthy inspiration of a natural life and controlled by that genuine criticism which came to them in the voice of the city.

3. But as the vigour of the Greek cities decayed, the citizen began to care less for the city and more for his private pursuits. **Social life became more and more separate from public life**, with which it had before been one. Among thoughtful men who did not engage in politics the old exclusiveness of Hellenic sentiment began to be modified. Such men began to ask not, *Is he a Greek citizen*?—but, *Has he a Greek mind?* This enlargement of intellectual sympathy—at the same time a sign of political decay—had first begun to show itself in the age of Epameinondas,

and, by its progress among the few, had helped to prepare the dissolution of Hellenic unity. It finds its clear and memorable expression in the words of **Isocrates**: 'Athens has brought it to pass that the name of Greek should be thought **no longer a matter of race, but a matter of intelligence**; and should be given to the participators in our **culture** rather than to the sharers of our common origin.'

4. The literature of Hellenism is no longer spontaneous or creative. It does not take its inspiration directly from life, but from books already existing. **The Hellenic literature was original: the Hellenistic literature is derivative.** Writers now appeal—not to the whole body of their fellow-citizens, as in the free Greek cities—but to the noble or learned few who, amid mongrel populations speaking mixed jargons, are the judges of Greek style. Literature becomes a polite industry, in which success is to be achieved by obeying or inventing critical canons. Mannerism and affectation begin to invade it.

5. **Alexandria**, the new capital of the Ptolemies, was the first great seat of literary Hellenism. Commerce quickly made its home at this natural centre of the traffic between East and West; and material wealth, in migrating from Greece to Egypt, drew the arts and sciences in its train. King Ptolemy I, surnamed Sôter, 'the Preserver' (306—285 B.C.), founded the **Museum**, or Temple of the Muses, which was somewhat like a modern university. The buildings included galleries of art, lecture-rooms and dining-halls. Distinguished men of learning were maintained at the Museum; and the beautiful gardens, with their shady walks, their statues and fountains, became famous as the haunt of Alexandrian poets and scholars. 'School after school, they had all walked and taught and sung there, beneath the spreading planes and chestnuts, figs and palm-trees. The place seemed fragrant with all the riches of Greek thought and song.'[1] The **Library** had once contained, in about 700,000 manuscripts, almost all that had been written in Greek; and even after the siege by Caesar, when part was burned, contained 400,000.

'There it towered up, the wonder of the world, its white roof bright against the rainless blue; and beyond it, among the ridges and pediments of noble buildings, a broad glimpse of the bright sea.'

6. In the Alexandrian literature, **Prose** holds the foremost place, and is especially employed in the labours of **science** and **erudition**. The ideal forms of the earlier Hellenic art can no longer be reproduced with freshness or success. **Poetry** either imitates these forms in a learned and scientific spirit, or seeks novelty in the by-paths of some lighter strain.

7. **Learned Poetry. Callimachus** (260 B.C.) has left six Hymns to the Gods, and a collection of epigrams; but his once famous elegies are represented only by fragments, and by the Latin translation of Catullus from his 'Lock of Berenice.' Berenice, the queen of Ptolemy Euergetes, had dedicated some tresses of her hair in a temple; they had been stolen; and the court-poet makes them relate how the gods had placed them among the stars. Ovid imitated his *Ibis,* a poetical invective against his pupil the poet Apollonius; and took the idea of the *Fasti* partly from his *Aitia* or 'Origins' of sacred tradition and usage. **Apollonius Rhodius** (194 B.C.) wrote the *Argonautica,* an epic in four books on Jason's 'Voyage in the Argo' to win the golden fleece. It is the work of a learned Homeric scholar who has not the Homeric feeling for the heroic age; it is artificial, and somewhat cold; but there is some fine dramatic painting; the poem is full of literary interest, and is the best of its class that the Alexandrian age has left. From **Lycophron** (260 B.C.), the most celebrated tragic poet of Alexandria, we have a poem called *Alexandra* in about 1400 iambic verses, in which Cassandra predicts how the voyage of Paris to Sparta will affect the fortunes of Asia and Greece. The mythology is obscured by far-fetched metaphor, and curiously illustrates the taste of the time for learned riddles in verse.

8. **Didactic Poetry. Aratus** (270 B.C.) was the author of an astronomical epic which Cicero translated, entitled *Prognostics*

of the Weather (*Diosêmeia*). It is from Aratus that St Paul, addressing the Athenians, quotes the words 'For we are also his offspring' (Acts xvii. 28). **Nicander** (150 B.C.) versified medical lore in two epics still extant,—one, called *Thêriaca,* on venomous bites, the other, called *Alexipharmaca,* on antidotes to poison. His lost *Georgics* were consulted by Virgil; and Ovid used his *Transformations (Heteroioumena)* as well as the *Metamorphoses* of the later poet Parthenius.

9. **Pastoral Poetry. Theocritus,** a Syracusan, flourished about 270 B.C. under Ptolemy II (Philadelphus), and is the Greek representative of **pastoral** or **bucolic** poetry. Shepherds contending for a prize in alternate or *amoebaeic* strains gave rise to this rustic poetry, which was distinctively **Dorian** and especially Sicilian; hence Milton call his *Lycidas,* in which one shepherd is supposed to be mourning for another, a *Doric* lay, and invokes the *Sicilian* muse. Besides some epigrams and fragments, we have 31 short poems under the name of Theocritus,—though the genuineness of some is doubtful,—mainly in the Doric dialect. Scarcely one half of these are properly *pastoral* in subject; but most of them may properly be called **idyls**, *i.e.* little pictures of life.[2] Here we see the **dramatic** influence of the Dorian farces or **mimes**, which Sophron made popular about 440 B.C.: especially in the 15th idyl, an amusing account of two Alexandrian ladies from Syracuse going to a festival. Much in Theocritus is artificial and conventional. But there is a true feeling for the sights and sounds of country life; the whisper of rustling leaves is in his poetry, the murmur of bees over summer flowers, the plashing of fountains in cool shades, the sunny brightness of the Sicilian sea. This, with his dramatic skill, might well commend him to dwellers in a city like Alexandria.

10. **Bion**, a native of Ionia, was another pastoral poet, best known to us by his Lament for Adonis, which Shelley has used in his *Adonais,* and which Mrs Browning has translated. The burden, 'Woe for Cytherea, beautiful Adonis is dead,' recurs at

intervals; such refrains are found elsewhere, as in the choruses of Aeschylus, in the first idyl of Theocritus, and in the exquisite lament of a third pastoral poet, **Moschus** of Syracuse, for the death of his master Bion. Few verses in Greek have more melody or more pathos than those in which Moschus sings that the glory of the garden fades to bloom again, but man, when he is once laid in the grave, sleeps an everlasting sleep.

11. **Parody** and metrical **satire** flourished in the Alexandrian age—springing, like the pastoral poetry, from a **Dorian** origin. Its most famous representative was **Timon** of Phlius (280 B.C.), who in his Parodies called *Silloi,* couched in hexameter verse, satirised all the dogmatic schools of philosophy.

12. **Prose—Philology and Criticism. Zenodotus** (280 B.C.), who became Librarian of the Museum under Ptolemy Philadelphus, entered upon the task of correcting and interpreting the texts of the Greek poets, especially Homer. He wrote memoirs of literary history, and compiled lists of rare words or phrases. **Aristophanes** of Byzantium (200 B.C.) extended his labours to the prose writers, and sought to preserve the true pronunciation of Greek,—which mixed populations were rapidly corrupting,—by introducing written signs to mark, in each word, the syllable on which the **accent**, *i.e.* the stress of the voice, ought to fall. **Aristarchus** (156 B.C.), by his effort to place textual criticism and interpretation on a basis of principles, became **the founder of scientific scholarship**. He rigorously revised the **canon**, or list of first-rate Greek writers in each kind, which his predecessors had drawn up. Admission to one of these select classes constituted what is still called a **classic**. One great work of these Alexandrian scholars and their followers—work known to us now chiefly from the fragmentary notices of later commentators—was **to establish a science of Grammar**. Under the name of **Apollodorus** (140 B.C.), a pupil of Aristarchus, we have a *Bibliotheca* or Library of Greek mythology in 3 books; which shows how the old literal belief in the myths had survived the attempt of EUHEMERUS (300 B.C.) to resolve them into fact or fiction.

13. Translation, especially of sacred books, was a province of the learned labour of Alexandria. The Greek version of the Hebrew Scriptures of the Old Testament was begun at Alexandria in the first half of the third century B.C., but was not completed before the end of the second century B.C. It was called the version of the **Septuagint** or Seventy, perhaps because it was authorised by the seventy members of the Jewish Sanhedrim.

14. **Science.** EUCLEIDES, or, as we call him, **Euclid**, was at Alexandria in the reign of Ptolemy Sôter, and gave Geometry a system in his famous *Elements*. ARCHIMEDES, who died in 212 B.C., the reputed inventor of the screw (*helix*), excelled in pure and applied mechanics. His contemporary **Eratosthenes** was the founder of astronomical geography and of scientific chronology. We have a piece of chronological work from the Alexandrian age in the *Parian Marble*, a summary of events in Greek history from the earliest times to 264 B.C., but available in its present state only to 355 B.C.

15. Chronology was combined with history by two writers who borrowed the Greek language of the governments under which they lived. MANETHO, an Egyptian priest in the reign of Ptolemy Philadelphus (285—247 B.C.), wrote Chronicles of Egypt. This work, of which only fragments remain, traced 31 dynasties down to the conquest of Egypt by Macedon. BEROSUS, *i.e.* Bar-Osea, a priest at Babylon in the reign of Antiochus Sôter (280—261 B.C.), carried the Chronicles of Chaldaea down to his own time. The authority of his work, based partly on the temple-archives, has been confirmed by a comparison of its fragments with the Old Testament.

16. Thus **the Alexandrian age busied itself with literary or scientific research, and with setting in order what the Greek mind had done in its creative time**. This spirit of many-sided labour lived on into the Byzantine age, producing histories, miscellanies, lexicons, down to the taking of Constantinople by the Turks (1453), when exiled Greeks began to spread the

knowledge of their language and literature more widely through Western Europe.

17. Greece became subject to Rome in 146 B.C. The result was to bring Rome into closer and more constant intercourse with the mind of Greece, and to begin that process, not completed till the time of Augustus, by which the political life of Hellenism was absorbed into the universal system of Rome. The first part of the **Graeco-Roman period** in Greek Literature extends to the close of the Roman Republic.

18. **Polybius**, the greatest Greek historian after Herodotus and Thucydides, stands on the border between the great Alexandrian age and that literature of which Rome was the central inspiration. He was born about 210, and died about 128 B.C. Seldom has so wide a variety of political experience been crowded into one life-time. His youth and early manhood fell on the days when the League of the Achaean cities was making its last stand against Rome. He was thus familiar with the earliest example of Federal Government—*i.e.* a league of communities in which each has control of its home affairs, but obeys a common authority in things which touch the common interest. His father Lycortas was captain of the League in 185—4 B.C., and came into office again when Philopoemen—the last hero of ancient Greece—died in 183. When the Romans had conquered Perseus, King of Macedon, Polybius was one of the 1000 Achaeans who were carried off to Rome. He was taken into the house of Aemilius Paulus, whose second son, the younger Scipio, was his friend; and, after 17 years, he procured the release of the other Achaeans. He was with Scipio at the destruction of Carthage in 146, and saw the burning of Corinth in the same year. The cities of the Achaean League then became subject to Rome, and Polybius was allowed by the Roman Commissioners to arrange the details of the new constitution (145 B.C.). He earned the gratitude of his countrymen; and statues in his honour were set up in several cities, including his native Megalopolis in Arcadia.

19. His **History**, in 40 books, was a record of Roman conquest from 264 B.C. to 146 B.C. We have only the first 5 books, and large extracts, or shorter fragments, of Books VI—XI. (1) Books I and II are introductory, linking on the History to that of TIMAEUS, which ended at 264 B.C. They deal chiefly with the First Punic War (263—241) and the Achaean League. (2) Book III carries the Second Punic War down to the Battle of Cannae (218—216); Books IV and V treat of Wars in Greece and Syria. The following books, to the 30th inclusive, traced Roman conquest to 168 B.C. The 31st to the 40th covered the period 167—146 B.C. Polybius used some Roman authorities, as the annalist Fabius Pictor; and Livy, from the beginning of the second Punic War, makes large use of Polybius.

20. *Rome,* says Polybius, *is the noblest and most beneficent work of Fortune.* But this 'Fortune' is no blind force; rather, in his own phrase, *an honest umpire,* an intelligent Providence, which has given the prize of empire to an imperial people. Polybius felt the inborn fitness of the Romans to govern. His own age decided that, as Greece was first in the things of the mind, so Rome was to rule the nations. The bent of his great work was to show that this was no accident, but the deliberate purpose of a wise Power. '*The whole earth subject to Rome*' is his vision. Yet he writes neither as a Roman, nor as a Greek who flatters Rome, but as a Greek with keen insight and a clear sense of harmony. Of earlier history he is not always a good judge; he shows that he did not understand the growth of the Roman constitution, and he misjudges Demosthenes; but he understood the lessons of his own wonderful age. He had known Achaia, Macedonia, Syria, Carthage all, in different measures, independent of Rome; and he had seen each in turn subdued by her. His **style** has been called 'a camp style.' It is plain, straightforward, sometimes rough; but it has not the faults of the contemporary rhetoric. His work has the further interest of being the oldest and best in the **common dialect**, based on the Attic, which dates from about 300 B.C., and is distinguished by a few peculiar forms, but chiefly by a less pure vocabulary.

21. All things gradually converged towards Rome. The learning of Alexandria and Athens was brought thither by the numerous Greek men of letters who found patrons or pupils in Roman families. From about 80 B.C., Greek literature, especially Rhetoric, became thoroughly established in the higher Roman education. The study of History and Geography also flourished.

22. **Diodorus Siculus** (40 B.C.) wrote a history of the world in 40 books, down to Caesar's Gallic Wars. We have only Books I—V, dealing with the early or mythical history of Egypt, Assyria, Aethiopia and Greece; and Books XI—XX, from the invasion of Greece by Xerxes (480 B.C.) to 302 B.C.; with fragments. This *Historical Library* was, as the title implies, less a single history than a series of histories, founded on the labours of predecessors, and grouped round the point which Polybius had recognised as henceforth the centre of political interests—Rome.

23. Historians had now ceased to produce original works with an artistic unity, such as those of Herodotus and Thucydides. Their aim was to present, in new combinations or more lucid arrangements, facts amassed by previous writers. This endeavour becomes the source of the most useful work which marks the closing centuries of the old literature.

Notes

1. Kingsley's *Hypatia.*
2. Virgil's similar poems, in which he occasionally imitates Theocritus, are called by the later name of *Eclogues,* 'selections,' a general name for short pieces.

8

FROM AUGUSTUS TO JUSTINIAN 30 B.C.—529 A.D.

Graeco-Roman period continued.—I. *History, Biography, Geography*: *Dionysius of Halicarnassus*, 25 B.C.; Plutarch, 90 A.D.; Strabo, 18 A.D.; Pausanias, 160 A.D. II. *Erudition*: Athenaeus, 190 A.D. III. *Rhetoric* and *Belles Lettres*: Lucian, 160 A.D.; Libanius, 350 A.D.; Heliodorus, 390 A.D. IV. *Philosophy*: Stoics: Epictetus, 90 A.D.; Marcus Aurelius, 170 A.D; Neoplatonists: Plotinus, Porphyry, Iamblichus, 250—300 A.D.; School of Athens: Proclus, 450 A.D. V. *Verse*: Babrius, 40 A.D.; Oppian, 180 A.D.; Nonnus, Quintus Smyrnaeus, 400—450 A.D.; Musaeus, 500 A.D.—Mystic poetry.—Anthology.—'Sibylline Oracles.'

1. Under the Roman Empire the Greek language and literature were diffused throughout the civilised world. Institutions resembling universities arose in the great cities. Teachers recognised by the State gave celebrity to the schools of Alexandria and Antioch, of Tarsus and Rhodes, of Pergamus and Byzantium, of Athens and Rome, of Marseilles and Lyons. The varied literature of Hellenism in the five centuries from Augustus to Justinian has four great departments: **History**, with the neighbouring provinces of Biography and Geography; **Erudition**, including grammar, criticism, archaeology and literary miscellanies; **Rhetoric**, in theory and practice, with kindred forms of ornamental prose, such as Dialogues, Novels and Letters; **Philosophy**, represented chiefly by Stoics and Neoplatonists. In Poetry there is little to record.

2. **History.** DIONYSIUS of Halicarnassus (25 B.C.), in his *Archaeology,* i.e. *Early History,* of Rome to 264 B.C. aimed at writing an Introduction to Polybius. He maintains, on fanciful grounds, that the Romans, who deserve to rule the world, are no 'barbarians,' but of Greek descent. We have Books I—X, going down to 450 B.C., and fragments of Book XI. He did a better work in his rhetorical writings, and above all in his excellent essays on the Greek orators. His object was to **revive a true standard of Attic prose**; and in this he was aided by his friend CAECILIUS, of Calacte in Sicily, who devoted himself especially to the province of verbal scholarship.

3. JOSEPHUS, of a noble Jewish family, wrote, in Greek the *Early History of the Jews,* to 66 A.D., in 20 books, on the model of Dionysius; and the *History of the Jewish War* in 7 books. The latter, his best work, extends from the capture of Jerusalem by Antiochus Epiphanes in 170 B.C. to its capture by Titus, which the historian witnessed.

4. ARRIAN, born about 100 A.D., and raised to consular rank by M. Antoninus Pius in 146, emulated Xenophon's *Anabasis* by relating the Asiatic Expedition of Alexander the Great in 7 books, of which we have all but the end of the 7th; and, after the example of Xenophon's contemporary Ctesias (a Greek physician at the Persian court) wrote, in the Ionic dialect, an *Indian History,* including the voyage of Alexander's general Nearchus from the mouth of the Indus to the Persian Gulf. And, as Xenophon preserved records of his master Socrates, so Arrian preserved records of his master Epictetus, who, like Socrates, left nothing written. From APPIAN (140 A.D.) we have still 10 books, besides fragments, of a History of Rome, divided according to the countries. HERODIAN (240 A.D.) has left a history of the Emperors from Commodus to Gordian (180—238 A.D.), in a style far from pure, but not without dramatic force.

5. **Biography.** PLUTARCH was born at Chaeronea in Boeotia about 40 A.D. He frequently visited Rome, and received honours from the emperors Trajan and Hadrian; but he never thoroughly

mastered Latin; and, though he could use Roman annalists, the only allusion to Roman poetry in all his works is a quotation from Horace in his life of Lucullus. Greece in his day had been almost drained of inhabitants; he tells us that the whole country could not put more than 3000 men in the field—the number sent in old days by one little town, Megara, to Plataea. It may have been partly the wish to remind the world that Greece could once breed as good men as Rome that led him to write his 46 **Parallel Lives**. These 'Lives' are in pairs, one Greek and one Roman in each pair. The ground of comparison is sometimes rather slight; thus *Alcibiades* and *Coriolanus* seem to be joined merely because both were slain in banishment. There are also four detached Lives—*Artaxerxes II* (Mnemon), *Aratus*, founder of the Achaean League, and the Emperors *Galba* and *Otho*. These Lives are vivid portraits of character, with some brilliant historical pictures. Plutarch was useful to Shakespeare (through North's translation) in the Roman plays.

The *Moralia* or 'Ethical Works' are a collection of about 80 pieces, by no means all on ethical subjects, but also on history, archaeology, and physical science. Some of the best ethical pieces are those on Garrulity, on False Shame, on Restraining Anger, on the Delays of Divine Justice. Among works wrongly ascribed to Plutarch are the 'Lives of the Ten Orators,' a 'Life of Homer,' and probably the collections of Apophthegms. These 'Sayings' are sometimes neat. There is one of a flute-player, with whom Philip of Macedon was arguing about music, replying, 'Heaven forbid that your Majesty should understand these things as well as I do.' Some Olynthian traitors complained to Philip that the Macedonians taunted them with having destroyed their native town. 'The Macedonians,' Philip answered, 'are boorish creatures; they call a spade a spade.'

6. **Diogenes Laertius**, who is usually placed early in the third century, in his eighty-four *Lives of the Philosophers*, deals with the early schools of Greek Philosophy, with the schools of Plato and Aristotle, and, in fuller detail, with Epicurus. Though

neither an accurate nor an elegant writer, he is often valuable as supplying information which is preserved nowhere else. FLAVIUS PHILOSTRATUS (235 A.D.), in his 59 *Lives of the Sophists*, gives us valuable material for the later history of Rhetoric. In his *Pictures* (*Eikones*) he has described 66 paintings of various classes, professedly from real works in a gallery at Naples, but more probably from his own imagination. Though essentially rhetorical in conception, this curious and once popular treatise is of much interest for art-history. *Appollonius of Tyana* (50 A.D.), whose *Life* Philostratus has written, was a renowned mystic, combining pythagoreanism with oriental magic, who in the third century received divine honours. The Emperor Alexander Severus placed the bust of this pretended miracle-worker in his Larium along with those of Abraham, Orpheus and Christ.

7. **Geography.** STRABO (18 A.D.) wrote a geographical work in 17 books, describing Europe (Bks. IV—X), Asia (XI—XVI), Egypt and Libya (XVII). His feeling is everywhere literary rather than picturesque; places interest him as the scenes of great deeds or because they are mentioned in great poems. PAUSANIAS (160 A.D.) has left a Tour of Greece in 10 books—(going through Attica—Corinth—Laconia—Messenia—Elis—Achaia—Arcadia—Boeotia—Phocis)—which is of the greatest value for the details of topography and the monuments of art. Somewhat in the spirit of Herodotus, but less simply and freshly, he seeks to bring out the *religious* meaning of all that he sees on this sacred ground of Greece. PTOLEMY (Claudius Ptolemaeus) of Alexandria (160 A.D.) built up a mathematical system of astronomy and geography which was universally received until, in the course of the 16th and 17th centuries, the system of Copernicus displaced it. Ptolemy believed that the sun, planets and stars revolved round the earth. His error in calculating the circumference of the globe warranted Columbus in supposing that the distance from the western coast of Europe to the eastern coast of Asia was about one-third less than it actually is; and thus encouraged the enterprise which led to the discovery of America.

8. **Erudition** continued to be fertile in the various branches of grammatical or critical work commenced at Alexandria. Among its products in this kind may be named the contribution to Greek lexicography made by JULIUS POLLUX in the second century. The physician GALEN (160 A.D.) wrote commentaries both on Plato and on Hippocrates, the founder of Greek Medical Science, whose works, in the Ionic dialect, belong to the close of the 5th century B.C. Galen's distinctive aim was to place medical science on a psychological basis by studying the affections of the body in connexion with those of the soul. ATHENAEUS (190 A.D.) represents a new and popular form of learned work. In his *Doctors at Dinner* (*Deipnosophistae,* in 15 books) he gives us a miscellany under the form of a conversation, which ranges over everything from Homer to cucumbers;—literature, natural history, medicine, manners, grammar. The work conveys some idea of the loss suffered by the destruction of the Alexandrian library. At least 700 authors are named who would otherwise be unknown. The *Stratagems* of POLYAENUS (170 A.D.) illustrate, by more than 800 anecdotes, the art of generalship, and occasionally of statecraft. From AELIAN (220 A.D.) we have a large collection of miscellaneous gleanings in history, biography and archaeology. The *Selections* and *Anthology* of STOBAEUS (480 A.D.) form another example; and a peculiarly valuable one is supplied, in the Byzantine age, by the *Library* of the Patriarch PHOTIUS.

9. **Rhetoric** was reduced to a complete system by HERMOGENES (170 A.D.). His work was long the standard text-book of an art which employed the best energies of the age. Early in the fourth century, however, it found a rival in the treatise of APHTHONIUS, which, at the Revival of Letters, once more became a favourite manual. CASSIUS LONGINUS (260 A.D.), one of the most accomplished Greeks of the third century, and minister of Queen Zenobia at Palmyra, has left a treatise on Rhetoric. To him is ascribed, though doubtfully, the essay 'On Sublimity,' one of the best pieces of literary criticism in the language. From the end of the first century A.D. rhetorical eminence became the chief road to public distinction. Chairs of

Rhetoric were posts of peculiar honour in the great cities of Asia and Europe. 'Even Thule,' cries Juvenal, 'talks of engaging an orator.'

10. Public teachers of Rhetoric were now officially distinguished by the name of **Sophist**, an old term revived in a special sense as an academic title, nearly equivalent, at this period, to the medieval 'doctor.' We have specimens of this new oratory from such writers as DION CHRYSOSTOM at the close of the first century; from AELIUS ARISTEIDES in the second; and, in the fourth, from THEMISTIUS, HIMERIUS and LIBANIUS: of whom the two last numbered among their pupils the Christian Fathers Gregory of Nazianzus, Basil and Chrysostom. The writings of another famous rhetorician of the second century, HERODES ATTICUS, are lost. LIBANIUS gives us some curious glimpses of University life at Athens and at Antioch. 'Some of them,' he says—referring to his disciples at Antioch—'stand like statues, with their arms folded on each other; others sit stock still, unmoved by my strokes of brilliancy or wit. Some try to interrupt those who feel stirred. Others vacantly count the numbers in the room; or stare at the trees that grow outside.' At Athens the students were organised in factions, and carried off a new comer by force to their favourite Sophist.

11. Rhetorical studies further helped to form an ornate literary prose, which took various light forms. LUCIAN (160 A.D.), a native of Samosata on the Euphrates lived to write Attic prose which, though by no means faultless, was the best that had been written for 400 years. His *Dialogues of the Gods*, almost Homeric in their freshness and almost Aristophanic in their fun, bring out the ludicrous side of the popular Greek faith; the *Dialogues of the Dead* are brilliant satires on the living. In his *Auction of Philosophers* the gods knock down each of the great thinkers to the highest bidder; Socrates goes for about £500; Aristotle for a fifth of that sum. In another piece, Lucian himself is tried for this jesting; but is acquitted, with the approval of Plato and others. Much historical interest belongs to his sketch

of *Peregrinus*, a man whom he represents as having been a Christian. Lucian notices several traits in the 'strange philosophy' of the Christians; their hope of immortality and their patience unto death; their holding of their goods in common; and their teaching that all men are brothers. His *Timon*, the misanthrope, is interesting in connexion with Shakespeare's play. The *Veracious History*, a mock narrative of travel, is the original of such books as *Gulliver's Travels*. Lucian has much in common with Swift, and more, perhaps, with Voltaire.

12. The Emperor JULIAN (b. 331—d. 363 A.D.) claims mention here, less for his extant orations or addresses than for his satirical pieces. His *Emperors, or the Banquet*, is a criticism, in the form of a dialogue, on his predecessors, in which Marcus Aurelius is extolled and Constantine disparaged. The *Misopôgon*, or *Beard-Hater*, is a satire levelled at the people of Antioch, who during a visit of Julian had insulted the opinions, and even the beard, of their sovereign.

13. The Greek **Romance**, or Novel, originated not later than the age of Augustus, and had two chief lines of descent. One of these was purely Greek, and is represented by XENOPHON the Ephesian (probably not later than 360 A.D.) in his elegant but somewhat frigid *Tale of Ephesus*, the love-story of Anthia and Habrocomes; and by the charming pastoral romance *Daphnis and Chloe*, which bears the name of LONGUS. The other series was influenced, through Syria, by oriental and especially by Indian fiction. Its best representative is HELIODORUS (390 A.D.). His *Tale of Aethiopia* relates the fortunes of Chariclea, a priestess at Delphi, and Theagenes, a Thessalian with whom she flies to Egypt. After many perils and separations they reach Aethiopia, and are on the point of being immolated to the sun and moon, when it is discovered that Chariclea is the daughter of the Aethiopian king,—having, by a miracle, been born white; and the union of the lovers is followed by the introduction of a more humane religion. ACHILLES TATIUS and CHARITON were inferior followers of Heliodorus.

14. Three books of fictitious *Letters*, written with vivacity in an artificial Attic style, bear the name of ALCIPHRON (about 180 A.D.). They represent a kind of literature popular from the beginning of the second century, and derive much of their material from the New Attic Comedy.

15. As the early Church grew in social power, it began to desire a counterpoise for the light literature of paganism. **Christian Greek Romances**, often written by Greek converts, were numerous from the beginning of the fourth century. Some of these romances related martyrdoms, historical or fictitious. Others were tales of monastic life. Others were imaginary journeys,—such as the 'Voyage of Macarius to Paradise.' Others had a controversial purpose. Thus *Abraham the Jew and the Merchant Theodore* was a plea for the worship of images. Theodore, ruined by a shipwreck and repulsed by his friends, borrows money from Abraham invoking, as his only security, the great Christ set up by Constantine in the copper-market before the palace at Byzantium. Again Theodore loses all, and again the Jew trusts him. Theodore sails westward, and this time prospers. Wishing to repay Abraham, but finding no messenger, he puts the money in a box, and commits it, in the name of Christ, to the waves. It is washed to the feet of the Jew on the shore of the Sea of Marmora. But, when Theodore returns, Abraham, to try him, feigns that he has not received it. Theodore requires him to make oath before the Christ. And as Theodore, standing before the image, passionately prays, the heart of his benefactor is turned to faith in the surety of the friendless.

16. **Philosophy**, during these centuries, is represented chiefly by the Stoics and the Neoplatonists. The Stoic School, with its unbroken Greek tradition from the beginning of the third century B.C., was distinguished under the Empire as that School which most earnestly sought to find a **practical rule** of life.

17. EPICTETUS, born at the Phrygian Hierapolis (a place mentioned by St Paul in his Epistle to the Church of the

neighbouring Colossae) was the sickly, deformed slave of Epaphroditus, a profligate and cruel freedman of Nero, afterwards put to death by Domitian for having done Nero the service of helping him to kill himself. There is a story of the master twisting the leg of his slave Epictetus, who said, 'If you go on, you will break it'; he did go on, and did break it, when Epictetus merely said, 'I told you so.' Later in life, Epictetus somehow got his freedom. He was driven from Rome by the edict of Domitian banishing philosophers in 94 A.D., and retired to Nicopolis in Epeirus, where Arrian was his pupil, and took the notes from which, nearly in his master's words, he has given us the *Discourses of Epictetus* (once in 8, now in 4 books), and the *Manual,* a summary.

The philosophy of Epictetus is Stoic with Socratic elements. Confining his attention to practical Ethics, he teaches that the beginning of wisdom is to discern between what is, and what is not, in our own power. The one thing which is in our power is to judge rightly—with the aid of a Guiding Spirit placed in us by God—concerning appearances (*phantasiae*), and so to secure our happiness by living in accord with Nature, that is, in accord with the divine order of the universe. Not in our power are all external things, such as poverty, failure, death. These things we must meet calmly. And we must abstain from all things likely to weaken the soul's power over the one thing which it *can* control. Hence the rule—'*Bear and forbear.*' Epictetus does not express belief in a future life. He holds that well-doing is its own reward. Man, he teaches, should always be content, knowing that God chooses for men better than they could themselves. 'In the place of all other delights substitute this,—that of being conscious that you are obeying God.' God brings man into life: 'and when he leads you out—after seeing the spectacle and the solemnity—will you not go out with adoration of him, and thanks for what you have seen and heard?'

18. As Epictetus dwelt rather on the moral dignity of man, so the Emperor MARCUS AURELIUS ANTONINUS (121—180 A.D.)

dwelt especially upon his need of divine support. Twelve books, written in Greek, contain the thoughts which he set down from time to time, and which are usually called his 'Meditations.' They do not show the Greek feeling for the beauty of goodness; they have not the subtle religious sense of the Hebrews; but they express, without enthusiasm, a humble and unfaltering reliance on a Providence which orders human affairs. In this religious philosophy God is at once a person and a law. He dwells in the human reason; man's first duty is to obey this divinity, this *'ruling faculty'* within him,—to keep it free from violence, above pains and pleasures; awaiting death as a breaking up of the elements that form man. Nothing can be evil that is 'according to Nature,' that is, according to God. Forgive injuries; all men are brethren; each must love and cherish the rest, and try to make them better, even when they wish him evil. The best revenge is, not to be like the wrong doer. This creed sustained Marcus Aurelius under domestic trial, and when, amid war and pestilence, he saw the Empire declining: nor should it be forgotten that he, like Epictetus, shows no clear hope of another life.

19. While Stoicism was thus pre-eminently a moral guide, **Neoplatonism** strove to seize the essence of knowledge and of existence. The oriental element traceable in Plato was developed at Alexandria, largely under Jewish influences, into a mystic doctrine. By ascetic discipline and intense contemplation the soul may achieve complete abstraction from the world of the senses, and may attain to complete union (*henôsis*) with God, the source of all knowledge. This doctrine, defined by Numenius (150 A.D.) and developed by Ammonius Saccas, was expounded in writing by the pupil of the latter, PLOTINUS (240 A.D.), who claimed inspiration and miraculous power, and averred that, four times during his life, in ecstatic trance, he had risen to the union with deity. His disciple and editor PORPHYRY, and the pupil of the latter, IAMBLICHUS, a mystic who forestalled the extravagance of a dervish, continued the laborious enthusiasm. It found a more gifted witness in the beautiful and noble-

hearted HYPATIA, who was cruelly murdered by the fanatic mob of Alexandria in 415 A.D.

20. In the fifth century calmer minds, still to be found in the **School of Athens**, made a last effort to rally the forces of Greek wisdom. PROCLUS (450 A.D.) sought to combine whatever was scientific in the conceptions of Neoplatonism with the best elements of earlier systems. The attempt failed: and his followers were equally unsuccessful. The victory of Christianity over the thought of the age was already all but complete when the edict of Justinian formally closed the schools of heathen philosophy (529 A.D.).

21. Meanwhile, for seven hundred years, the higher **Poetry** had been almost silent. BABRIUS (40 A.D.) put into choliambic verse the Fables ascribed to Aesop, whose legendary date is about 560 B.C., but from whom we have no authentic remains. Plato describes Socrates in prison amusing himself by putting such fables into verse. 'The Wolf and the Lamb' is a fair sample of the skill of Babrius, who was freely translated into Latin by PHAEDRUS. OPPIAN (180 A.D.) wrote the *Fisher's Art* (*Halieutica*), a clever epic of the didactic sort in 5 books, on the habits of fish and the modes of capturing them. He is also the reputed author of the epic on *Hunting* (*Cynegetica*), in 4 books,—greatly inferior to the other, but with some good descriptions. Buffon consulted it. NONNUS, early in the fifth century, gave epic poetry a short, flickering life; his huge epic *On the Adventures of Dionysus* is a romance of physical nature,—fervent, but often turgid, and showing an Egyptian taste for crude colour. QUINTUS SMYRNAEUS (450 A.D.) wrote a sequel to the *Iliad* in 14 books, carrying it down to the capture of Troy; and though devoid of poetical originality, is of value for the study of Homer. Under the name of MUSAEUS (500 A.D.?) we have 340 verses, of much beauty, on the story of Leander swimming the Hellespont to see Hero.

22. Poetry of a **mystic** character forms a special province of the later Greek verse. The *Argonautica* (which must be distinguished from the poem of Apollonius Rhodius) is an epic

in 1384 lines, written probably in Egypt before 400 A.D., and treating select incidents in the voyage of Jason. ORPHEUS, bard, prophet and enchanter, is the central figure: his mysterious power over the world of gods, spirits and men is the central motive of the whole. The *Lithica*, in 768 hexameters, composed probably soon after the death of Julian in 363 A.D., celebrates the talismanic properties of rare or precious stones, and vindicates magic science from the disrepute into which it is falling. The eighty-seven *Hymns*, sometimes styled 'Orphic,' can have nothing in common with the Orphic hymns which old Greek writers mention in connexion with an Orphic ritual. The hymns in our collection represent the tendency of the later Neoplatonists to resolve the old Greek deities into abstract or mystic formulas; and few of them, perhaps, are older than 350 A.D.

23. The **Greek Anthology** brings together epigrams and short pieces ranging over about 1000 years,—from Simonides of Ceos (490 B.C.) to the sixth century of our era. MAXIMUS PLANUDES, a monk of Constantinople (1330 A.D.), put together a collection, founded on that of AGATHIAS (550 A.D.), in seven books. This was the only one till, in 1606, the scholar Saumaise, better known as Salmasius, found a manuscript in the library of the Elector Palatine at Heidelberg, containing another Greek Anthology, put together by Constantinus CEPHALAS, about 920 A.D. This is now known as the **Palatine** Anthology; and it is now seen that Planudes had, in large measure, merely rearranged or abridged it. Love, art, mourning for the dead, the whole range of human interests and sympathies, lend leaves to this garland of Greek song.

24. Early Christian writers occasionally quote the **Sibylline Oracles**, regarding these, apparently, as genuine utterances of a heathen prophetess who sometimes became the involuntary mouth-piece of divine truth. **Sibyl** (usually explained as 'Counsel of Zeus') was a name given by the Greeks to an inspired being with various local habitations. The mosaic pavement of the

Cathedral at Siena represents the whole series of famous Sibyls, and illustrates the recognition accorded by the earlier Church to this pagan vehicle of revelation—whose testimony the old funeral hymn, 'Dies irae,' associated with that of David. The 'Sibylline Books' of Rome—said to have been brought by the Sibyl to Tarquin, and consulted in times of difficulty by the Senate—were destroyed by fire in 82 B.C. A new collection was then put together from Sibylline books preserved in other places. This second collection, after several revisions, was finally burned in the reign of Honorius (395—423 A.D.). The existing 'Oracles,' in Greek hexameter verse, are by Jewish or Christian writers, ranging in date from about 170 B.C. to 700 A.D., who seem to have aimed at reproducing certain traits of style or form—such as the use of acrostics—which belonged to the old Sibylline oracles. We have twelve of the fourteen books once extant: books IX and X are lost. The third and fifth books express, in the form of prophecy, the Jewish longing—quickened by the visible decline of Hellenism under Alexander's successors—for a political Restorer of Israel. Other books predict the history of the world from the Flood (in I and II, probably the latest of all, the Sibyl is the daughter-in-law of Noah),—foretell the triumph of Christianity,—and allude to the belief that Christ shall reign on earth for a thousand years.

25. As the literature of Greek culture had gradually lost its significance, a constantly greater importance had accrued to the **Greek Literature of Christianity**, represented by the Epistles, Homilies and learned works of the Fathers, and by Ecclesiastical Histories such as those of EUSEBIUS, SOCRATES and SOZOMEN. The relations between the declining and the rising literature passed through two great phases. The Christian writers who immediately succeeded the Apostolic age, true to its example, had not ignored either the humanising value of Greek letters or the theological interest of Greek thought. Justin Martyr, Origen and, above all, Clement of Alexandria had in their different ways claimed recognition for the endeavours of the Greek search after truth.

26. But towards the end of the third century a different spirit began to appear. While Neoplatonists like Plotinus alleged that philosophy had anticipated revelation, Christian writers like Eusebius maintained that whatever was good in Greek thought had come to it through the Hebrew Scriptures. The progressive estrangement of the Christian laity from Greek letters, and the divergence of spoken from written Greek at Constantinople, were the two great causes which in the fourth century hastened the decay of literary Hellenism. Yet the greatest Christian Fathers of that century, Gregory of Nazianzus, Basil, his brother Gregory of Nyssa, and Chrysostom were trained by Greek masters in the art of expression—that art in which all men still felt the power of ancient Greece; and the matured eloquence of the preacher first issued from the schools of Antioch and Athens.

27. In the Christian Greek Literature of the Middle or Byzantine period (529—1453 A.D.) the classical beauty of form and purity of style disappear. Learned writers, generally ecclesiastics, compile annals, works on Grammar, Mathematics, Medicine, miscellanies or criticisms of the Old Literature; while by the side of these labours a school of popular poetry at last springs up,—unlike the classical poetry in form and spirit,—and links the Medieval on to the Modern Literature.

For 350 years after the capture of Constantinople by the Ottoman Turks (1453) the Greeks had small hope of regaining independence. Their efforts were concentrated on doing what they could to save their nationality from being effaced: above all, on preserving the two things by which it was chiefly marked —their language and their religion. Hence the Greek literature of those centuries was mainly occupied either with philological studies of the old Greek writers, or with Theology. Gennadius, the first Patriarch after the Turkish conquest, founded at Constantinople a 'National School' which did much to keep alive the higher culture through a difficult time, and which, before 1700, had become famous. From 1716 onwards the

Sultans appointed Fanariots—*i.e.* Greeks of Constantinople, so called from the quarter of the city in which they lived—to govern the two Roman Principalities of Wallachia and Moldavia; and the courts of these Fanariot princes became centres of encouragement for Greek literary effort.

Then, at the beginning of this century, hopes of freedom began to stir. Far-seeing friends of Greece such as Koraes helped to restore the purity and vigour of the language, and so to render it a more efficient instrument of national regeneration. A new literary energy set in. From 1800 to 1821 this had chiefly a preparatory purpose: there was not as yet a social life to which it could be practically applied. The War of Independence, which began in 1821, led in 1827 to some—not all—of the Greeks becoming free. Liberated Greece had first to organise education: the next impulse was to make up lost way by translating foreign books into Greek. During the last fifty years Greek writers have contributed to almost every province of letters, especially to Philology, Archaeology and History : and there is good reason to hope that the literature of Greece—in its recovered vigour, still so young—will continue to enrich the language that it inherits.[1]

28. The great original work of the Greek mind in art and literature had been done before 300 B.C. But a wider, if a less brilliant, activity remained for it. Rome, as a Roman poet says, made the whole earth to be one people. And as this was done by the military and political genius of Rome, so, within the iron framework which she wrought, **a universal culture** was animated by the elastic intelligence and interpreted by the flexible language of Greece. From **Rome,** along with a noble literature, the modern world derives a continuous tradition of **law and government**: from **Greece** it traces the ancient lineage and the still fresh inspirations of an **intellectual and spiritual life.**

Note

1. An excellent survey of the period from 1453 to the present-day will be found in the 'History of Neo-hellenic Literature' by A.R. Rangabé (Berlin, 1877).